Effective Knowledge Management

Other titles currently available in the *CBI Fast Track* series:

Strategic Decision Making by George Wright
Radical Process Change by Ashley Braganza
Managing Workplace Stress by Stephen Williams & Lesley Cooper
Business Driven HRM by David Hussey

Effective Knowledge Management

A Best Practice Blueprint

SULTAN KERMALLY

JOHN WILEY & SONS, LTD

Other Wiley Editorial Offices

John Wiley & Sons, Inc., 605 Third Avenue,
New York, NY 10158-0012, USA

WILEY-VCH Verlag GmbH, Pappelallee 3,
D-69469 Weinheim, Germany

John Wiley & Sons Australia Ltd, 33 Park Road, Milton,
Queensland 4064, Australia

John Wiley & Sons (Asia) Pte Ltd, 2 Clementi Loop #02-01,
Jin Xing Distripark, Singapore 129809

John Wiley & Sons (Canada) Ltd, 22 Worcester Road,
Rexdale, Ontario M9W 1L1, Canada

British Library Cataloguing in Publication Data

A catalogue record for this book is available from the British Library

ISBN 0-470-84449-3

Typeset in 11/15.5pt ITC Garamond Light by Footnote Graphics, Warminster, Wiltshire
Printed and bound in Great Britain by Biddles Ltd, Guildford and King's Lynn.
This book is printed on acid-free paper responsibly manufactured from sustainable forestry, in which at least two trees are planted for each one used for paper production.

Contents

List of Case Studies:
Real Companies

1. J D Edwards
   Customer Support Service based in High Wycombe

2. Knowledge=Power Ltd

3. The Scotch Whisky Association

4. NatWest Life

5. Simon Jersey Ltd

6. Carousel Nurseries

7. Costain

8. Sainsburys

9. Xerox

10. Yamazaki UK Ltd

11. Strachan & Henshaw

Series Foreword

I am delighted to be able to introduce to you the *CBI Fast Track Series*. The book you are holding is the outcome of a significant new publishing partnership between the CBI and John Wiley & Sons (Wiley). It is one of the first in a long line of high-quality materials on which the CBI and Wiley will collaborate. Before saying a little about this partnership, I would like to briefly introduce you to the CBI.

With a direct corporate membership employing over 4 million and a trade association membership representing over 6 million of the workforce, the CBI is the premier organisation speaking for companies in the UK. We represent directly and indirectly, over 200 000 companies employing more than 40% of UK private sector workforce. The majority of blue-chip organisations and industry leaders from the FTSE 250 are members, as well as a significant number of small to medium sized companies (SMEs).* Our mission is to ensure that the government of the day, Whitehall, Brussels and the wider community understand the needs of British business. The CBI takes an active role in forming policies that enable UK companies to compete and prosper, and we ensure that the lines of communication between private and public leaders are always open on a national scale as well as via our regional networks.

The appropriateness of a link between the CBI and a leading business publisher like Wiley cannot be understated. Both organisations have a vested interest in efficiently and effectively serving the needs of businesses of all sizes. Both are forward-thinkers; constantly trend-spotting to envision where the next issues and concerns lie. Both maintain a global outlook in servicing the needs of its local customers. And finally, both champion the adoption of best practice amongst the groups they represent.

Which brings us back to this series. Each *CBI Fast Track* book offers a complete best practice briefing in a selected topic, along with a blueprint for successful implementation. The aim is to help enterprises achieve peak performance across key disciplines. The series will continue to evolve as new and different issues force their way to the top of the corporate agenda.

I do hope you enjoy this book and would encourage you to look out for further titles from the CBI and Wiley. Here's to all the opportunities the future holds, and to *Fast Track* success with your own corporate agenda.

* Foreign companies which maintain registered offices in the UK are also eligible for CBI membership.

Digby Jones
Director-General, CBI

THE VOICE OF BUSINESS

About the author

Sultan Kermally holds degrees in geography, economics, sociology and law (from Scottish and English universities), diplomas in finance and accounting and marketing, and a Certificate in Further Education.

Professionally he is a freelance management development consultant, trainer and coach designing and delivering training and development courses in business strategy, developing newly appointed managers, leadership and motivation, managing people, managing performance, managing knowledge and personal effectiveness. He has conducted training for well-known companies in the UK, the Netherlands, Belgium, France, Italy, Austria, the Middle East, Hong Kong and Tajikistan.

For several years he held senior academic positions in Scotland and thereafter senior management positions with Management Centre Europe in Brussels, London Business School and The Economist Intelligence Unit, where he held the position of Senior Vice President of the Economist Conferences, Europe.

At Management Centre Europe and at the Economist, Sultan spent a considerable time working with well-known management 'gurus' including Peter Drucker, Michael Porter, Tom Peters, Richard Pascale, Philip Kotler, Rosabeth Moss Kanter, Benjamin Zander and Tony Buzan.

He has been involved in management education and development for number of years, including distance learning management education courses. He has been tutoring with the Open University and Open University Business School since their inception. He is an associate lecturer in strategy and knowledge management for the Open University Business School MBA modules. He also teaches organisational behaviour, international business and human resource management MBA modules for the Durham University Business School.

He is the author of *Total Management Thinking* (1996), *Management Ideas* (1997) and *Managing Performance* (1997), all published by Butterworth-Heinemann in association with the Institute of Management; *When Economics Means Business: The New Economics of the Information Age* (2000), published by FT Management; *The Management Tool Kit* (1999), published by Hawksmere; and *New Economy Energy: Unleashing Knowledge for Competitive Advantage* (2001), published by John Wiley.

He is currently undertaking one-to-one performance coaching assignments with senior and newly appointed managers at Volkswagen Group HQ based in Milton Keynes.

For consultancy, coaching and training assignments, Sultan can be contacted at:

57 Southlands Road
Bromley
Kent BR2 9QR
Tel: +44 (0)208 313 3378
Fax +44 (0)208 460 1536
E-mail: Skermally@aol.com

Acknowledgements

This book would not have been possible without John Moseley, Publishing Editor at John Wiley. John's confidence in my ability to write a book on knowledge management in association with the CBI is very much appreciated. He has also been very supportive in his approach. My sincere thanks to him.

The following individuals and organisations have also contributed to my efforts directly and indirectly:

- John Wiley & Sons, Ltd.
- The Fit for the Future team for their support and for allowing me to use their case studies.
- TSO Consulting, which specialises in strategy, leadership and performance, and in particular Lyn Bicker, managing director and Rachael Bicker, director of operations and research, for hosting knowledge management seminars for their clients.
- The Open University Business School for giving me an opportunity to teach the Managing Knowledge MBA module course.
- Celemi's president and CEO Margareta Barchan for allowing me to reproduce an interesting article on measuring intangible assets.
- The American Productivity & Quality Center for granting me permission to reproduce a case study on Xerox Corporation.
- *Marketing Week*.
- The Wiley production team in particular Viv Wickham and Sally Lansdell for their professionalism.
- Thanks and love to my wife Laura, a knowledge worker herself, for her constant encouragement, my daughters Zara (allowing me to gain an insight into development stages), Susan (for her coping mechanisms) and Jenny (for her appetite for knowledge), my son Peter (for his down-to-earth approach to life), my grandchildren Matthew, Anna and Eve (for their happiness) and my son-in-law Thomas Powell for his pride in my work.

Introduction:
Managing Knowledge
Without Tears

Managing knowledge involves creating an environment within an organisation that facilitates the creation, transfer and sharing of knowledge. The focus, therefore, is on creating an appropriate organisational culture and providing effective leadership.

Knowledge is becoming very important in gaining and sustaining competitive advantage. Some organisations believe that knowledge is for big businesses only and that small enterprises, simply because of their size, do not need to do anything about managing knowledge.

In fact, knowledge management does not discriminate as far as the size of the enterprise is concerned. It is very important for all businesses, whatever their size or sector.

The Purpose of this Book

This book is aimed at clarifying certain myths that exist about managing knowledge and explaining how organisations can manage knowledge without tears.

The content is presented with a 'best practice' approach. What is advocated is what organisations should do in order to compete effectively in a changing and complex business climate.

Frequently asked questions

1   Is knowledge management a fad?

No, it is not. Knowledge is one of the key intangible assets an organisation possesses. Increasingly the products and services of many organisations consist of ideas and innovations. Knowledge management is here to stay.

2   Is knowledge management new?

Knowledge management is as new as Egyptian pyramids. Various civilisations in the past have managed knowledge to establish their positioning and to thrive in their respective communities. We have gone through various stages of economic development, from agricultural economy to industrial economy and recently the information economy. It, is simply that more organisations are paying attention to managing knowledge now because of the complexity of business and the convergence of technology.

3   Is knowledge management important for small businesses?

Intangible assets consisting of customers and employees are important for all businesses. Such a question would not arise if the nature of managing knowledge were understood.

4   What is knowledge management?

It is about creating an exciting environment within the organisation that will promote the creation and transfer of knowledge.

It is about changing corporate culture and about visionary leadership, motivated staff, loyal customers and the systems and processes that facilitate these things.

5   Do we need to recruit experts to introduce knowledge management?

There is no need to recruit expensive experts. In the beginning of a knowledge management initiative it will help to bring in outside help, but the outsider should work as a facilitator and then phase

CONTINUED ... Frequently asked questions

out gradually so that the employees within the organisation can own and sustain the initiatives.

6   Do we need to invest heavily in IT?

No, most of the initiatives can be started by very little investment in IT. Technology should be used as an enabler.

This book explores various initiatives that can be started without initially spending any money on IT. Managing knowledge is about managing people, not technology.

7   Which is the best knowledge management system for small businesses?

There are many knowledge management system vendors, but they are not concerned with knowledge management as such. Systems enable the capture of information; they do not enable knowledge creation. Only you as a leader can motivate your staff to create and transfer knowledge.

8   Can benchmarking help to introduce a knowledge management culture in the organisation?

Benchmarking is about adopting and adapting best practice. Best practice in relation to becoming an effective leader or to improve customer service or to develop your staff leads to an appropriate culture for managing knowledge.

9   Many consultants and books on knowledge management give examples of best practice in relation to global and large national organisations such as Sony, Xerox, Chevron, McKinsey, Ernst & Young, Microsoft and so on. Are there examples of small firms from which one can learn?

This book has used cases from CBI resources focusing on best practice in relation to various aspects of business management.

CONTINUED ... **Frequently asked questions**

These best practices will lead organisations to start to think about managing knowledge.

10   What techniques and approaches can one adopt to start managing knowledge?
This book examines various approaches to making a start and shows how to leverage and measure intangible assets.

Chapter 1 looks at the concept of best practice and how one goes about conducting benchmarking of best practice. The emphasis in this chapter is on the process of benchmarking and a step-by-step approach.

Chapter 2 considers the challenges that all types and sizes of businesses face in the twenty-first century. It reflects on how these challenges can be met and how to monitor external changes that affect business.

Chapter 3 explores the nature of managing knowledge and its importance to various businesses. The chapter examines why some organisations are reluctant to manage knowledge. Attention is also given to the importance of managing knowledge for small businesses.

Chapter 4 looks at processes that have to be put in place in order to facilitate knowledge creation and transfer. Various initiatives are proposed to enable organisations to make a start.

Chapter 5 deals with the role of technology and emphasises the fact that the Internet is now removing industrial boundaries, so that small as well as large organisations are well positioned to take advantage of its capability.

Chapter 6 explores the importance of leadership in managing knowledge. Building corporate culture, recruiting and retaining staff and empowering staff are presented as key attributes of the modern leader.

Chapter 7 looks at what constitutes intangible assets and how organisations can use their intangible assets to build their competitive capability.

Chapter 8 addresses issues of measuring intangible assets. The Business Excellence Model, the Balanced Scorecard, the Skandia Navigator and the Intangible Asset Monitor are introduced as frameworks of measurement that could be considered by organisations. These frameworks can be customised to meet business needs.

Chapter 9 focuses on making a start. Cases of both global and small companies are given to show how organisations can identify best practice and undertake organisational auditing to prepare to become knowledge-driven organisations.

Chapter 10 is a short reminder in a form of an A to Z of knowledge management.

The format adopted is a best practice approach devoid of jargon and pragmatic enough to be of use to business executives.

Best Practice Winning Formula

An interview with a marathon-winning high-performing athlete

Q: What makes you a high-performing athlete?

A: I have stamina, strength and a will to learn.

Q: What is the difference between you and other athletes?

A: I take care of myself. I develop my internal resources and convert them into capabilities.

Q: What do you mean by your internal resources?

A: I mean my stature, my physique, my energy, my attitude, and most importantly my hunger to become the best performer.

Q: What preparation do you do before taking part in a marathon?

A: I train, train and train. I also consider the state of my health and I get information on competition, my near competitors and general environment.

Q: What kind of information do you collect on competition and competitors?

A: I gather information on who they are, what are their achievements and where. What type of environment we will be running into etc.

Q: At a personal level what things do you consider?

A: Apart from training I also consider the type of footwear and clothing appropriate for the racing conditions. These enable me to achieve my objectives.

Q: What do you do after you gather information?

A: I use the information to my advantage.

Q: Do you become complacent after winning so many races?

A: No. I treat every race individually and I continuously make an attempt to improve my performance.

Q: Do you get any help from anyone or do you do everything yourself?

A: No, I rely on my coach to feed me with information and bounce my ideas off him. Coaching is one of the ingredients of my success.

Q: What would your advice be to young people who would like to copy you?

A: Train to become fit. Have the right attitude and you must also have an ambition to win. Do your homework in relation to where you are going to compete, your external environment and your competitors. Use your coach to help you. Always be prepared for a new race. Learn from best performers.

Moral of this interview

To be the best in class consider your strategy, your structure, your mindset, your resources and capabilities, your external factors and your competitors, and gather information to convert it into knowledge that you could use to gain and sustain competitive advantage.

Continuous improvement and emulating best practice should be the culture of your organisation.

ONE

Best Practice Transfer:
A Business Imperative

If British companies adopted only the average best practice levels of leading competitors, the UK's annual GDP would increase by £300 billion. (Fit for the Future campaign web page)

Overview

- Improving business and organisational performance should be one of the key strategic objectives of every organisation.
- The Internet age has removed the boundaries of industries and now small and big businesses compete within the same market place and market space.
- Best practice transfer, therefore, has become the business imperative of big organisations and SMEs (small and medium-sized enterprises).
- Benchmarking is one of the key ways of introducing a best-practice mindset in your company.
- Benchmarking is a process and it involves various steps that should be considered properly.
- There are many types of benchmarking that organisations can undertake.
- If an organisation is not comfortable with benchmarking against other best-practice organisations, it can create its own model of best practice to benchmark against.
- The benefit of best practice transfer is to achieve quantum leap changes without reinventing the wheel.

> **CONTINUED ... Overview**
>
> • Benchmarking creates organisational knowledge that can be transformed into organisational capability.

The concept of best practice applies to every kind of organisation, big and small, for profit and not for profit. The concept is also applicable in practice to the way in which businesses manage their people,

> **KEY CONCEPT**
>
> The concept of best practice applies to every kind of organisation.

their customers, their partners, their operations and their processes.

This book is a guide to adopting best practice in the area of managing knowledge

There are many ways of adopting best practice. One way of doing so is to use benchmarking. This is not a new method and it has been in existence for several years. However, it is a widely used tool and in some cases it is not used to the best advantage.

Organisations want to achieve and sustain high levels of growth and profitability. To do so under very intense competitive pressures they have to examine the way they manage their business, the way they treat their people, the way they satisfy and delight their customers, the way they deal with their suppliers and other partners, the way they operate and use various processes.

> **KEY CONCEPT**
>
> Benchmarking enables organisations to import best practice.

Benchmarking enables organisations to import best practice in different aspects of business.

A word of caution

Benchmarking is about *adopting and adapting* the best ways of managing business. Straightforwardly 'importing' techniques or methods may damage your business, however.

What is benchmarking?

Benchmarking is a means of improving business or organisational performance. It is a way of identifying the work processes of industry leaders that represent best practice and adopting and adapting these processes to your situation with a view to gaining superior performance.

It is, in essence, a change programme that enables the achievement of best practice. According to the CBI, it is the most effective way of doing business.

Digby Jones, Director General of the CBI, comments:

Our research suggests Britain can increase GDP by £300 billion if it adopts the average best practice levels of leading competitors...

One thing I've learnt is that the best practice concept applies across the board. It doesn't matter whether you're in traditional manufacturing or the service sector, high tech or low tech, what really matters is that you are receptive to new ideas and willing to learn from others. No one knows it all. Whether you're in a company striving to achieve best practice or spreading the message to others – keep in touch with this major CBI initiative and make us all 'Fit for the Future'.

> **KEY CONCEPT**
>
> The best practice concept applies across the board.

Launched with the support of the Department of Trade and Industry and led by the CBI, Fit for the Future arose from a desire to make the UK more productive and globally competitive. It encourages an open exchange of ideas and expertise in order to help companies revolutionise the way they work. Its mission statement is: 'To achieve a massive increase in the number of companies engaged in the transfer of best practice.'

Fit for the Future works through a partnership network of companies and

> **KEY CONCEPT**
>
> Fit for the Future works through a partnership of companies.

organisations that believe in the value of best practice. It points companies to valuable sources of information and advice. It also helps raise the profile of its partners' best practice activities.

The following information is provided on the CBI website:

Fit for the Future is not about re-inventing the wheel. Quite the opposite. The aim is to add value and weight to the host of existing initiatives by raising the profile of best practice work and by encouraging different industry sectors to talk to and learn from each other.

The transfer of best practice is crucially important because it really is a powerful tool to help companies achieve valuable productivity and competitiveness gains. Fit for the Future will make a difference. The question is, how much of a difference? The answer to that is very much dependent on the commitment, motivation and enthusiasm of every one involved. (Alec Daly, chairman, Anite Group plc and Founder chairman of the Fit for the Future Steering Group).

British Prime Minister Tony Blair has endorsed this campaign:

I am sure that Fit for the Future will continue to gain momentum, as it promotes a powerful message that organisations can achieve substantial business improvement through learning from their peers.

Benchmarking as a process should be continuous and systematic and it should involve evaluation and measurement. The process is the cornerstone of organisational improvement.

Early experience of benchmarking was in the manufacturing sector because manufacturing output is intangible and measured *(what gets measured gets managed)* and the focus of benchmarking was on process. Gradually the technique came to be applied more generally to processes, products and people as well as to various functions such as finance, logistics, research and development and managing people.

Below is the example of one medium-sized textile company that undertook a benchmarking exercise on different aspects of business with various other companies.

- *Textile company* The way this company paid attention to people management.
- *Manufacturing company* The way this Company paid attention to quality
- *Retail Company* The way this company was handling logistics.
- *Finance company* The way this company was handling its billing and collection.

These companies were selected because they had a reputation of 'best practice' in relation to certain aspects of their businesses.

Before undertaking benchmarking do consider the following:

 ## BENCHMARKING

- Why do you want to benchmark?
- What is it you want to benchmark?
- What specific outcomes are you expecting?
- How are you going to measure these outcomes?
- Are there best performers you can learn from and how would you identify them?
- What type of organisation would you like to benchmark against?
- What type of information would you like to collect and how are you going to collect it?
- Who are you going to involve in your benchmarking team and why this choice?
- Who are going to be the 'benchmarking champions'?
- What do these individuals get out of being involved in this process?
- How are you going to monitor whether the work is being done right?
- How are you going to communicate results?
- How are you going to bring about the desired change?

How to Benchmark: Creating Organisational Knowledge

Step 1 Identify subject to benchmark

It is very important as a first step to identify what it is you are going to benchmark. It could be that you want to improve your fulfilment service or your logistics or you want to improve your billing and debt collection service, or your delivery performance or the way you compensate your staff and so on. You must know exactly what it is you are after at this stage.

Let us assume that you want to improve your customer service as far as quality and delivering your product or service are concerned. First of all, determine the present level of satisfaction of your existing customers.

You can do this by asking your customers their views of your service by way of questionnaires (postal/telephone/on your website); conducting interviews with your customers; or hiring specialist consultants to do this for you.

You must find out the existing level of customer satisfaction in order to effect improvement. This involves mapping your processes and all the activities involved in each process that forms part of delivery to customers.

Planning is very important at this stage. It is also important to determine the scope of the benchmarking exercise you propose to undertake. Focus on the operation that is within your scope and

> **KEY CONCEPT**
>
> Planning is very important at this stage.

resources. If you do not do this you will, like many other organisations, waste your time in gathering information that you will not be able to do anything with. If you do not use the information then you have not created any knowledge at all.

You also have to deal with many stakeholders at this stage. Stakeholders are individuals or groups who have a direct interest in your business, such as your employees, your shareholders or your investors.

In conducting customer satisfaction benchmarking, your accounts department may want you to focus the study on the billing process; your marketing department may want you to focus on the way the customers receive communications from your organisation; your customer care department may want you to focus on the complaints volume and procedure.

At this stage, decide what your priorities are and what resources you can allocate.

Step 2 Identify best practice

Identify which organisation has the reputation of best practice in customer service. Break down customer service into different aspects such as speed and manner of delivery, the way complaints are handled, on-time delivery, after-sales service, repeat business etc. Focus on some of these aspects at the initial stages.

It is also important that in identifying best practice you do not focus on numbers alone. For example, do not simply look at the number of complaints without examining the way in which the complaints are handled. In other words, consider the processes involved behind the best practice.

> **KEY CONCEPT**
>
> It is also important that in identifying best practice you do not focus on numbers alone.

Step 3 Collect Information

Having determined the organisation or department against which you want to benchmark, start collecting information on different aspects of customer service.

These first three steps come under the planning stage of the benchmarking process.

Step 4 Analyse data collected and transform data into information

Transform this data into information. How do various aspects of customer service of the organisation against which you are benchmarking compare with your organisation? How do its processes for dealing with various aspects of customer service, such as complaints, differ from yours? Determine the gaps and conduct gap analysis. Build organisational knowledge of the areas that require improvement.

Step 5 Issues to address

Even though you may have decided on the scope of the project, do decide at this stage how and what issues to address in order to close the gaps. Decide on your performance indicators towards the achievement of best practice.

Your performance indicators should be selected with care, otherwise you could be measuring an inappropriate achievement.

For example, Express Parcel Delivery chose as one of its indicators speed of service. It benchmarked this indicator against its key competitors and found out that it had the best achievement in this area. It achieved the fastest delivery of parcels to its customers. However, in spite of this record and the low volume of customer complaints, Express found out that it was losing customers. On further investigation, it established that the customers did not like their service compared to its competitors because in meeting the delivery time target, its staff did not have time to be friendly to its customers.

In deciding on performance targets consider the following:

- They are appropriate.
- They measure what you want them to measure.
- They are reliable.

> **KEY CONCEPT**
>
> Formulate appropriate, reliable and measurable targets.

Step 6 Prepare a strategy for action

Once it is prepared, communicate this strategy to your staff, all those involved in bringing about improvements in customer service.

Step 7 Action plan

Develop an action plan covering who is to do what and by when.

Step 8 Implement your plan and set target dates

Appraise the situation to see if you are on track. If not, revisit your objectives and fine-tune them.

Step 9 Recalibrate the benchmark

Check that it is giving you the information you need and if not adjust it.

Step 10 Undertake a performance review

Review the targets and indicators set and record the findings.

Benchmarking is a continuous and systematic process. The best practice is to plan the project according to the steps highlighted above. Implement the process and monitor it continuously. Take appropriate action to incorporate changes and return to the continuous improvement cycle for guidance (see Figure 1.1).

In steps 7 to 10 you have to make use of the information collected by taking appropriate action to adopt best practice. If you do not do anything with information then you have a passive asset. Interpreting information and doing something with it is how you create knowledge

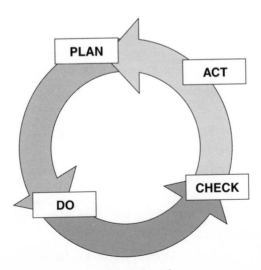

Figure 1.1 *Continuous improvement cycle*

and using this knowledge (the intangible assets of your organisation) will bring about the desired results.

Steps 9 and 10 involve examining this knowledge and how to leverage it to improve your organisational performance and establish your reputation as a best practice organisation.

Some organisations are sceptical about benchmarking. They say (a) it is expensive; (b) it is better to lead than follow the leader; and (c) there is a danger of benchmarking inefficient aspects of business.

Benchmarking is not expensive. It has been said, 'If knowledge is expensive, try ignorance.' Secondly, the whole rationale of benchmarking is to be the best in the sense of adopting best practice. You cannot lead if you do not have best practice in your organisation. Once you do become a best practice organisation, then let other organisations benchmark against you.

> **KEY CONCEPT**
>
> If knowledge is expensive, try ignorance.

Finally, if you have done your planning properly there is no danger of adopting inefficient practices. Planning involves not just SMART but SMARTER principles.

 BENCHMARKING

S: *Specific.* Specify your objectives very clearly and be very specific about them.

M: *Measurable.* What gets measured gets done.

A: *Attainable.* Make sure you are not too ambitious if this is your first attempt.

R: *Relevant.* Your objectives should be appropriate to your desired outcomes and they should be realistic.

T: *Time specific.* Decide on a date by which you want to achieve your objectives.

E: *Entrepreneurial.* Your objectives should encourage individual thinking and action.

R: *Recorded.* Your objectives should be in writing in order to minimise or avoid misunderstanding.

What Are the Benefits of Benchmarking?

Benchmarking for best practice:

- Provides direction and impetus for improvement.
- Makes you look inside and outside your organisation.
- Provides you with information that you can turn into knowledge in order to enhance your capability to compete effectively.
- Involves staff in generating ideas to bring about improvement.
- Promotes competitive awareness.
- Provides an opportunity to collaborate.
- Makes you aware of your organisational weaknesses.
- Triggers a major step change in business performance.
- Challenges the status quo.
- Enables you to review your competencies.
- Achieves breakthroughs and promotes innovation.
- Enables the organisation to create knowledge that, when used, becomes organisational capability.

Types of Benchmarking

So as we have seen, improvements are made and knowledge is created by undertaking various types of benchmarking, which we will now discuss in more detail.

Internal benchmarking

You do not have to go outside your organisation to identify best practice. For example, an automotive group based in Europe represents five brands of cars. Each brand is housed in a separate division. One particular division has acquired a best practice reputation in dealing with its dealers. Other divisions decided to benchmark against this best practice.

This exercise was not easy, however. A desire to protect one's turf, a suspicion of copying to spend less money, spying, internal politics, different union representation and so on created barriers to access. In the end, nevertheless, good leadership and open communication overcame these barriers and the group as a whole benefited from the internal benchmarking.

Internal benchmarking has the following advantages:

- It establishes organisation-wide best practice.
- It promotes open communication.
- It encourages collaboration.
- It brings about change in organisational culture.
- It can establish common practice and standards.
- It has a favourable impact on costs.
- It promotes an understanding of the nature of benchmarking.
- It instils confidence in undertaking external benchmarking should this prove necessary.

Competitive/external benchmarking

This involves benchmarking against competitors who have a reputation as a best practice organisation. It may be difficult to get information on your competitors, but there are many examples in practice of organisations willing to cooperate and collaborate.

There are benchmarking 'clubs' and partnerships being formed to encourage companies to undertake best practice external benchmarking. In the UK, the DTI and CBI facilitate benchmarking for different kinds and different sizes of organisation.

> **KEY CONCEPT**
>
> In the UK, the DTI and CBI facilitate benchmarking for different kinds and different sizes of organisations.

It is very important to treat the information from external sources with respect and always to work on the basis of the way you would like your information to be treated by others.

Process benchmarking

This type of benchmarking can be undertaken at an internal or external level. The processes can be compared internally with other group members or other departments or divisions, or externally with other organisations' processes.

One department store, for example, benchmarked against a supermarket food chain to compare the range, design, source, distribution, display and sales, all the components constituting supply chain management.

Functional benchmarking

Benchmarking can also be undertaken to improve or enhance specific functions. For example, one organisation benchmarked against another organisation's way of dealing with people management, specifically in the recruitment and training of staff.

Another organisation benchmarked against the role played by a finance director in another organisation with a view to improve the effectiveness of the finance function.

A popular practice is to undertake customer service benchmarking with a view to providing service excellence.

Benchmarking without emotions

Some organisations are not keen to benchmark against best practice organisations because they feel that such a practice may produce information that could adversely affect staff morale and motivation. One way out of this situation would be to create a model of best practice.

Avon Products Inc. is the world's leading seller and marketer of beauty related goods. The annual turnover in 1994 was in excess of $3.5 billion and it marketed its products in more than 100 countries through 1.5 million independent representatives.

Avon is also the world's largest manufacturer of fashion jewellery. The trigger point for them was to review their business with their customers. They used a service quality survey method called 'servqual' which measured customer

expectations and perceptions from which they identify gaps.
(Kermally, 1996)

One small organisation gathered its staff together to brainstorm and design the type of organisation they would like it to be. They focused their attention initially on the following:

- The type of staff they would like to have.
- The level of customer satisfaction they would like to achieve.
- The nature of the relationships they would like to have with their partners.
- The level of financial performance they would like to achieve.

Brainstorming produced some key attributes of such an organisation and from this 'desired organisation' the company undertook a benchmarking process. It identified significant gaps that it subsequently took action to close. The advantage of such an approach is that it involves staff and undertakes benchmarking without threat.

 PAUSE FOR THOUGHT

- Being the best involves continuous examination of your products, processes and people, which are your intangible assets.
- Best practice incorporates an organisational willingness to learn and adapt.
- Best practice provides a platform for becoming a knowledge-driven organisation.
- Benchmarking is not an end but a means to an end. It is what organisations do after benchmarking that matters.

How Can You Obtain Information?

The biggest challenge facing many organisations in undertaking external benchmarking is to know where and how to get information.

There are many ways of obtaining information. Below are some sources of information that may help:

- Annual reports.
- Press reports.
- Customer feedback.
- Market research reports.
- Trade associations.
- Academic case studies.
- Books.
- Competitors' advertising.
- Former employees.
- Benchmarking clubs.
- Joint venture partners.
- Site visits.
- Conferences.
- Government data.
- Industry experts.
- Salespeople.
- Distributors and suppliers.

Identifying industry best practice is a powerful focus for change. It is also said that quality of service is never an accident; it is the result of intelligent efforts. Benchmarking enables organisations to improve their capabilities and win and sustain competitive advantage.

Best Practice Transfer

Organisations have been talking about best practice transfer for a number of years. Some believed that such a practice was only appropriate for big and global businesses. However, the world has changed significantly and these changes now directly affect all businesses, big and small.

Best practice transfer is not an option any more. The next chapter surveys the changing business landscape and how, in

> **KEY CONCEPT**
>
> Best practice transfer is not an option any more.

order to remain competitive and sustain your competitive advantage, it is important that you embark on best practice transfer.

Whether best practice transfer is successful or not will depend on the vision of your leadership, your commitment and your understanding of and response to changes in a business environment. Best practice transfer has now become a business imperative for all types of business – big, medium and small.

TWO

Creating Organisational Knowledge of External Changes

We are indeed in the early stages of a major technological transformation, one that is far more sweeping than the most ecstatic of the 'futurologists' yet realize, greater even than Megatrends *or* Future Shock. (Peter Drucker)

Overview

- The business world is being globalised.
- Globalisation affects all types and sizes of business.
- It incorporates trading blocs such as the World Trade Organisation (WTO) and the European Union.
- It should be viewed as an opportunity for businesses.
- Driving forces of globalisation are changes in sociological, technological, economic and political factors.
- These changes should be scanned and monitored and their impact on your business should be analysed.
- This will enable you to build information that can subsequently be transformed into knowledge of your competitive as well as external environments.
- Globalisation has been reinforced by the emergence of the new economy and e-businesses.
- Scenario planning is an important tool today.

All organisations, irrespective of size, have to operate and make business decisions within the context of changes taking place outside their organisations at national and international level. These changes have favourable and unfavourable impacts on business operations. It is therefore important to understand and appreciate *how* these changes affect your business.

We live and do business in a global market place. Recently the owner of a small grocer's shop pointed out to me how globalisation has affected his business. He now has to import mangoes from India, bananas from the Caribbean, coffee from Kenya and Uganda, oranges from Israel and so on. This is a clear indication of how trading in a global market place has an impact on the way you do business now.

> **KEY CONCEPT**
>
> We live and do business in a global market place.

Globalisation

The term 'globalisation' was coined in the 1980s to mean the economic interdependence of countries. It effects a fundamental transformation of the structures and nature of international trade. The process of globalisation influences the way we trade, our trading partners, the skills required to compete in such an environment, the creativity and innovation of organisations, the job situation, our environment, cultures and values. It is, therefore, an all-embracing phenomenon.

The collapse of Communism and almost universal support for market economies, combined with technological developments and an explosion in information, have encouraged a far greater trend towards globalisation than before.

Globalisation means that some businesses can now choose to manufacture goods in one country and sell them in others, constantly looking out for efficient locations.

The focus of globalisation from a business perspective is on trade and competitiveness. As far as trade is concerned,

> **KEY CONCEPT**
>
> The focus of globalisation from a business perspective is on trade and competitiveness.

globalisation triggers bring down trade barriers on an international scale.

After the Second World War 23 countries met at Geneva to establish a forum for trade liberalisation. They signed the General Agreement on Tariffs and Trade (GATT), its main objectives being the reduction of tariffs and the promotion of free trade over the years. Between the first and second rounds of GATT talks, approximately 50 000 tariff concessions were negotiated. By 1995 tariff cuts affected over $300 billion worth of world trade.

In 1994 the World Trade Organisation was established to cover trade agreements relating to goods, services, intellectual property and a new dispute-settlement mechanism. So when the US and the European Union are in dispute over bananas, the World Trade Organisation acts as a dispute-resolution body.

Case Study: Dispute between America and Europe

The following case was reported in the *Economist* of 8 May 1999.

Friction between the world's two trading countries which do trade of around $400 billion a year with each other.

There has been a long standing conflict over bananas and beef. On April 6, 1999 the WTO ruled for the third time that the European Union must amend its banana-import rules which discriminate unfairly against American fruit distributors. On April 19th, 1999 the WTO gave America the go ahead to put retaliatory sanctions against $191 million of European imports.

The WTO has also ruled that the European Union must lift its ban on hormone-treated beef by May 13, 1999 because there is no convincing scientific evidence that the hormones are dangerous.

Tariff reductions, subsidies, import licensing and intellectual property protection do not exclusively affect big international companies. Theses actions affect SMEs as well.

Various trading blocs such as the European Union and the North Atlantic Free Trade Association (NAFTA) have come into existence to reinforce the liberalisation of trade and promote economic integration.

European Union

In 1957 the Treaty of Rome was signed creating the European Economic Community, consisting of Belgium, the Netherlands, Luxembourg, the Federal Republic of Germany, France, the Netherlands and Italy.

In 1973 the United Kingdom, Ireland and Denmark joined followed by Greece in 1981 and Spain and Portugal in 1986. In 1992 the European Economic Community (EEC) became the European Union. In 1995 Austria, Finland and Sweden became members. Other countries want to join, especially Turkey, the Czech Republic, Slovakia, Poland, Hungary and the countries of the former USSR.

The European Union, according to the International Monetary Fund, is the largest import and export market in the world and it accounts for 20% of world trade.

In 1992 the European Union began creating the Single Market to facilitate the free movement of goods, services, capital and labour. The Single Market was meant to increase competitiveness within Europe.

> **KEY CONCEPT**
>
> The European Union is the largest import and export market in the world and it accounts for 20% of world trade.

The European Union has also set the goal of achieving a single currency among its members. In 1990 the European Commission convened an Inter-governmental Conference on Economic and Monetary Union. The objective was to discuss the steps to create monetary union under a single currency. The first draft was completed in Maastricht and it has ever since been referred to as the Maastricht Treaty.

The timetable for monetary union under a single currency was planned to take place in three stages:

- Stage one began in 1990 with the lifting of controls on the movement of financial capital within the European Union.
- Stage two began in 1994 with the creation of the European Monetary Institute based in Frankfurt in Germany.
- Stage three began in 1999 with the creation of the European Central Bank.

Before becoming a fully fledged member of the monetary union each member country has to satisfy five convergence criteria. These are:

- Stable exchange rates.
- Low inflation.
- Harmonisation of long-term interest rates.
- Reduction of government deficits.
- Reduction in government debt.

In 1999 the European Union introduced the single currency, called the euro.

Some of the pros and cons of the single currency are as follows:

Pros
- It removes the costs and uncertainties associated with intra-European trade.
- It strengthens competitive pressures.
- It increases the range of investment opportunities.
- It reduces the costs of currency conversion.

Cons
- Europeanising the labour market will increase costs.
- The euro has proved a volatile currency because of the market uncertainties.
- It involves restructuring of business, especially banking business.
- Individual nations cannot pursue their own independent policies.

It should be noted that the UK has decided not to join the move to a single currency for the time being. At the time of writing neither Prime Minister Tony Blair nor Chancellor of the Exchequer Gordon Brown wants to reveal his hand about when exactly the government might recommend that Britain should join the euro.

Britain first has to pass the convergence tests and then the government will have a referendum. It is speculated that the referendum will be held some time in the middle of 2003.

Apart from the WTO and the European Union there are other regional blocs affecting trade patterns, such as the North American Free Trade Agreement (NAFTA) and the Association of South East Asian Nations (ASEAN).

European Business and Globalisation

Globalisation is an opportunity for Europe to seize, not a threat. Far from being the cause of unemployment in Europe, it is a potential source of employment creation. There is a close link between the development of world trade, economic growth, and employment. A major part of the Union's prosperity today is based on trade and international investment. But to make the most of it and obtain maximum benefit in the interests of Europe's citizens and economy, the Union must adjust to this new state of affairs without delay and equip itself with the best means for capitalising on it. (Commission of the European Communities, 1999)

> **KEY CONCEPT**
>
> Globalisation is an opportunity for Europe to seize, not a threat.

The driving forces of globalisation are technological advances such as the convergence of computing and telecommunications and the advent of the Internet, political initiatives in relation to the privat-

> **KEY CONCEPT**
>
> All organisations, multinationals and SMEs, must adopt best practice to be able to compete in the global market place.

isation and deregulation of financial and other markets, and the escalation of cross-border capital flows such as bank lending, international bond issues and mutual fund portfolio investments.

Globalisation increases competitive pressure, which reinforces a Darwinian principle that only the fittest will survive. To be 'fit for the future' all organisations, multinationals and SMEs, must adopt best practice to be capable to compete in the global market place.

What can organisations do with all the information on changes happening in their business environment? The best practice would be to capture these changes and create organisational knowledge. That knowledge can then be used to prepare strategies under different scenarios and to respond to market changes and needs to come up with innovative products and services to gain competitive advantage.

The way to capture changes is to conduct an analysis of those taking place external to your organisation.

How to capture external changes

Step 1

First, categorise these changes under the headings of social, technological, economic and political factors (STEP factors).

Social changes relate to changes taking place in society, such as changes in attitudes, values, educational systems, population, the role of groups such as women, population mix and so on.

Among these social changes, identify those that affect your business directly. For example, in analysing social changes an insurance business identified the ageing population of Britain as one of the significant changes affecting its business. It came up with appropriate products for this market segment.

Technological changes affect the diffusion of technologies in our society. Technological developments are taking place at a breathtaking pace, specifically in the telecommunications and entertainment industries. Satellite technology is creating a global broadcasting system, for example. The convergence of computing, communications and information is leading to global information superhighways that expand markets, develop new businesses and increase competition.

Electronic commerce is a catalyst synonymous with greater market transparency and immediate global competition. Even in traditional labour-intensive industries, it is a powerful driver of change and an incentive to competition. It favours the diffusion of varied products and services as well as developing the diversity of European know-how and Europe's productive base. For SMEs, market niches, their traditional targets, can now be exploited globally. Innovative start-up companies and SMEs can have access to global markets and acquire an international dimension from the beginning. (Commission of the European Communities, 1999)

Technologies are enabling even very small business to compete effectively with big businesses. According to Gary Hamel, a strategy guru:

> **KEY CONCEPT**
>
> Technologies are enabling even very small business to compete effectively with big businesses.

In a garage somewhere an entrepreneur is forging a bullet with your company's name on it. If you lead a large company with a history stretching back decades, the chances are that small start-up is going to relegate you to the third division, if not to extinction. (Hamel, n.d.)

Decide which technologies affect your business directly. For example, Ford Motor decided to use the Internet to unleash radically new ways of doing business in order to compete in the new economy. Companies, big and small, are now conducting on-line operations to take advantage of the Internet revolution.

So decide both on the technology you would like to use and on how you are going to use it to improve your business.

Economic factors affect economic decisions taken by governments or groups such as the European Union: decisions to change interest rates, policies to control inflation and employment and so on. Many small businesses, for example, feel that high interest rates are affecting their bottom line and they are constantly expressing their views to try to prompt the government to consider the position of small businesses.

Consider what economic changes affect your business directly and how. For example, changes in interest rates affect the building trade, especially private housing market. Higher exchange rates affect the cost of doing businesses for many companies.

Political factors include all those decisions taken by government to increase competition, such as bringing down trade barriers, getting rid of political ideologies, privatisation, deregulation and so on.

For example, the deregulation of the airline industry directly affected the key players in this industry. It enabled budget airlines such as easyJet and Ryanair to come into existence and increase competition in the airline industry.

Consider which political factors are going to affect your business, and how.

Many organisations arrange brainstorming sessions with their staff to consider these social, technological, economic and political factors so that staff are involved in the analysis and become aware of these changes in the environment affecting their businesses.

Step 2

Having considered and isolated STEP factors, conduct an impact analysis on the basis of the probability of change and the impact on your business, as shown in Figure 2.1.

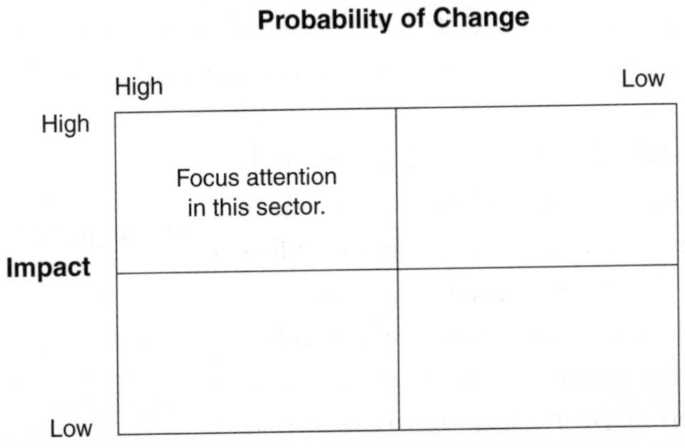

Probability of Change

Figure 2.1   *Impact analysis*

Step 3

The factors that fall in quadrant A have a high probability of change and also a high impact on your business focus on this area.

Step 4

Prepare your strategic plan according to this analysis.

In analysing these factors you may consider various scenarios for your business, especially as the business climate is becoming very complex and competition very intense.

Undertaking scenario planning is best practice for an organisation. It is often said that scenario planning is only for global businesses like Shell and that it is an old-fashioned way of preparing strategic plans. This is not the case, as the following example makes clear.

 PAUSE FOR THOUGHT

Of course we made mistakes. The biggest was our expansion into America. But we had an awful lot of bad luck at home: two hot summers which depressed hosiery sales, combined with a series of train and tube strikes which kept so many of our shops closed one day each week over several months. And on top of that, interest rates doubled to 15 per cent. Any one of these factors we could have coped with but not all of them together. And there was absolutely nothing we could do about any of them. I felt like a rabbit caught in headlights. (Sophie Mirman, Sock Shop, in Barrow, Brown and Clarke, 1992)

This is the tale of a small business that could have gathered information on likely external changes and acted on this information to prepare scenario planning to deal with 'alternative futures'. *This is what knowledge management is all about – interpreting and using information to make business decisions.*

> **KEY CONCEPT**
>
> This is what knowledge management is all about – interpreting and using information to make business decisions.

Scenario planning is *not* about predicting the future. Scenario planning is about the flexibility of the organisation to deal with changes. It is about adopting best practice in proactive thinking and strategy. Scenario planning has become very important, especially in new-economy enterprises.

> **KEY CONCEPT**
>
> Scenario planning is about the flexibility of the organisation to deal with changes. It is about adopting best practice in proactive thinking and strategy.

Some businesses feel that undertaking STEP analysis is costly and time-consuming. This should not be your attitude. Undertaking STEP analysis is one of the best ways to create organisational knowledge and it is not a cost but an investment. Once this type of knowledge is created it appreciates every time it is used.

Case Study: We can do it

'ResearchNet' is a publishing company employing 250 people. The organisation is divided into several departments, such as editorial, finance, marketing and sales, printing and fulfilment. It is a small company with very limited resources.

However, the managing director of this company decided to build organisational knowledge on changes affecting her company. She wanted to undertake a pilot study and start creating knowledge of external changes by asking marketing staff to set the ball rolling.

The marketing manager decided to involve all his staff by asking me to bring in information on any change outside the organisation that would affect it.

An individual was asked to record the change on a Post-it note™ and stick it on a departmental noticeboard. Every week one person, appointed as change coordinator, would collect and collate this information. At the end of a month this person would prepare a short report highlighting the changes and present this report for discussion and action to the monthly staff meeting.

CONTINUED ... Case Study: We can do it

This gradually grew into a very useful exercise because (a) it involved all the staff; (b) it used resources effectively to capture external changes; (c) the exercise became meaningful to the staff and inherently motivating; and (d) changes were introduced in an evolutionary way, without traumas.

As a result of this practice changes were instituted by this department in order to respond to market needs.

Other departments emulated the best practice of this department and very soon it spread throughout the organisation. Today 'ResearchNet' prides itself on preparing plans incorporating various scenarios and the whole culture of the organisation has changed to become collaborative.

Best Practice in the New Economy

The new economy is characterised by e-businesses, most of which are very small. For these businesses e-strategy is key to their future success. The following article provides best practice advice on strategy and scenario planning.

> **KEY CONCEPT**
>
> The new economy is characterised by e-businesses, most of which are very small.

E-strategy is key to future success

By Sultan Kermally

Internet-based companies are the new business model for the future, despite the downturn in high technology share prices and boom and bust in the dot-com economy. Multiple visions for the future and more emphasis on scenario planning are just two of the prerequisites for strategic success.

The beginnings of e-business lie in the origins of the internet which has opened up all kinds of business possibilities. It has enabled organisations to reduce costs, enhance revenues, make real-time contacts and achieve market stretch.

When leading American business entrepreneur Jack Welch, of General Electric, was asked if he considered internet-related business to be important, he indicated in the affirmative and when asked how and where he would rank the internet in his business strategy, he said: "Number 1, 2, 3, 4 and 5."

It is estimated that more than 200 countries are connected to the internet and two hundred million people can access it. Even in China it is reported that twenty-three million users now have access to the internet. In a very short space of time it has become the most powerful tool of business transformation.

> **KEY CONCEPT**
>
> It has been said that no technology in history has spread faster than the internet.

Many established business leaders are cynical about transforming their businesses into e-businesses. This cynicism is based on failures of many dot-com companies and poor performance of technology shares.

However, the internet is clearly with us and here to stay. Businesses have to seriously consider the arrival of the new economy and consider strategies to operate within the new macro-economic environment.

The internet-based company now represents a new business model with its own unique value chain. It is predicted by some experts that European e-commerce will surge to one trillion pounds sterling by 2004. There have been some casualties and there will be more but this should not deter businesses from adopting e-strategy.

Established businesses like Pirelli, Ford and General Electric have developed e-business strategies and are trading on-line. They have to embrace e-business in order to deal with the complexity of the new business environment.

According to Gary Hamel, the strategy guru, the competition these days is not between products but between new business models.

The new business model requires the following characteristics:

- Flexible value chains – configured constantly to meet the challenge of rapid change and business complexity.
- Entrepreneurial mindset – throughout the whole organisation and led from the top.
- Knowledge management – the key driver.
- Strategic focus on creation of multiple futures – scenario planning takes centre stage in the new business model (see dos and don'ts section).
- Strategic partnerships – a business imperative, together with outsourcing.

It is important to remember that the new business model has no room for 'default strategy', which focuses on a single approach to strategy and a single view of the future.

E-businesses with all the right characteristics have the following attributes. They are:

- On-line (doing business over the internet).
- Responsive to customer needs (competition is only a click away).
- Have visionary leadership.
- Gain global reach with very limited resources.
- Ensure every link in the value and supply chain is networked.
- Have blurred organisational boundaries and a tolerant and collaborative culture.

The e-business model is important because it:

- Makes it possible for information to be shared more quickly and easily.
- Facilitates human interaction.
- Enables organisational resources and capabilities to be stretched strategically.
- Provides global reach in marketing, transforming the market place into the market space.

- Allows consumers to shop 24 hours a day from any location.
- Promotes economic growth.

Becoming an e-business is now a business imperative for all types of organisations, large and small. The key success factor lies in not emulating established habits.

> **KEY CONCEPT**
>
> Becoming an e-business is now a business imperative for all types of organisation.

Leadership in the new economy needs to:

- Enthuse employees.
- Empower and respect employees.
- Create trust throughout the organisation.
- Understand the importance of knowledge as a source of business energy.
- Identify and leverage intangible assets.
- Be a custodian of corporate governance in the age of the internet.
- Be willing to engage in 'constructive destruction', since e-business requires constant renewal of its business model.

Creating scenarios embraces a process that is very interactive, intense and imaginative. It involves challenging the mental models that shape our perceptions and behaviours.

Apart from scenario planning, e-businesses also have to focus on paying special attention to recruiting and retaining staff.

Superior financial performance in the new economy depends significantly on intellectual capital. That well-worn phrase 'our people are our greatest asset' will become a reality.

It is important not to become complacent about adopting e-business. The longer you leave it, the longer it will take to catch up with competitors. E-business will give your organisation more speed to respond to changes in the external environment. It will enable organisations to share the business 'vision' and knowledge very effectively and it will give greater access to customers.

It will also enable partnerships and network relations to flourish – a crucial factor in the new business economy.

Source: Sultan Kermally, *Professional Manager* (September 2000), published by the Institute of Management. Reproduced by permission of *Professional Manager*.

Scenario planning – dos and don'ts

Scenario planning, originally developed within Royal/Dutch Shell, is about making better business decisions today in order to compete more effectively tomorrow. It enables organisations to anticipate surprise in a changing business world. According to one guru, a good scenario is not whether it portrays the future accurately but whether it enables an organisation to learn and adapt.

Do:

- Consider the STEP factors (sociological, technological, economic and political) surrounding your business environment.
- Conduct an impact analysis of these factors. Consider the probability of change and how they will impact on your business.
- Construct various scenarios. Three or four carefully constructed scenarios should suffice.
- Create multiple futures facing your business.
- Question your mental models.
- Plan for and anticipate surprises.
- Adopt a multi-disciplinary approach.
- Make the scenario constructing process interactive and imaginative.
- Assume a 'what if' mindset.
- Create a collaborative culture.
- Involve all staff.
- Propose strategies appropriate to various scenarios.

- Work out the action plan in relation to each scenario. This will transform your business from being reactive to proactive.
- Implement your action plan.

Don't:

- Embark on this exercise without conviction and commitment from the top management.
- Get stuck into 'one best strategy'.
- Work on existing assumptions.
- Simply gather information on STEP factors without using it to convert into business knowledge.
- Build numerous scenarios without moving to strategy. Too much analysis can lead to paralysis.
- Prepare a plan without identifying who should do what, how and by when.
- Conduct a scenario planning exercise as a one-off event.

Source: Taken from *Professional Manager* (July 2001), published by the Institute of Management. Reproduced by permisssion of *Professional Manager*.

Building Organisational Knowledge on Competition and Competitors

Apart from building knowledge on external environmental factors, organisations should also regularly undertake analysis of their competition and competitors.

Analysing your competition and your environment

 BENCHMARKING

- Find out who are the key players in your industry.
- How many key players are there?

- Which players affect your business most and why?
- Which players are known for best practice and in what area?
- Consider benchmarking against this player.
- Collect information on products, processes and people.
- Try to collect information on its customers.
- Consider the likelihood of new firms entering your market.
- What are the main barriers to entry?
- What are the substitutes available that affect your business?
- How can you differentiate your product/service against competitors?
- Who are your main suppliers?
- Can you form partnerships with your main suppliers?
- Who are your key customers?
- How can you improve your relationships with your key customers?
- What type of customer service do you provide?
- Do you have staff to deliver service excellence?

This is good old competitor intelligence, which some consider to be old hat. The problem in practice has been that many organisations gather information and leave it in their *organisational attic*. For you to be a high-performance organisation this information has to be converted into knowledge and the organisation has to use this knowledge to compete effectively.

If they do this, small and medium-sized enterprises can play a significant role in the new economy in creating employment and enhancing growth.

Digital networks lower the cost of entry to world markets. In the USA, the digital economy is building on the critical mass of SMEs and innovative, networked start-ups. Fuelled by easy access to capital at every stage of their development, these enterprises are able to rapidly leap from a simple idea to world leader in this field. Despite having three times as many SMEs as in the US (15 million versus 5 million), Europe is lagging behind in this process.

KEY CONCEPT

Despite having three times as many SMEs as in the US (15 million versus 5 million), Europe is lagging behind in this process.

The creation of employment is at stake. In the US two thirds of new jobs created over the past four years were in high-tech companies, half of them in SMEs. In Europe 50% of new jobs were created by a fast growing group of 4 per cent of Europe's SMEs. (Commission of the European Communities, 1999)

High-tech companies are experiencing some downturns at the moment, but SMEs can still play a key role in enhancing business and consequently economic performance if they set their mind to adopting best practice management and use personal and organisational knowledge effectively. The importance of managing knowledge is addressed in the next chapter.

THREE

The Importance of
Managing Knowledge

You cannot manage knowledge; you can only manage the environment that leads to the knowledge being created and transferred. (Anon)

Overview

- All businesses have to formulate strategy.
- Changes outside as well as inside the organisation should be considered when preparing a strategy.
- Resources and capabilities play a key role in the type of strategy you are going to adopt.
- Adopt a best practice approach to preparing your strategy.
- Do not ignore people-related and other 'soft' issues that constitute your organisational capabilities.
- Knowledge is one of the key intangible assets that can help you gain and sustain competitive advantage.

All businesses have to have a strategy in relation to what it is they want to do, how they want to do it and the time scale involved. This is what business strategy is all about. Strategy is also related to how businesses gain and sustain superior performance.

In preparing a strategy the following key questions have to be addressed:

- What business is the organisation in?
- What products or services does it want to provide?

- What markets should it target?
- What are the skills and capabilities it has that it can use to achieve its objectives?

In answering these questions the focus is not only internal but also external. In other words, organisations have continually to monitor and respond to changes happening outside their environment and inside their industry.

> **KEY CONCEPT**
>
> Organisations have continually to monitor and respond to changes happening outside their environment and inside their industry.

Changes in economic climate, nationally and internationally, changes in technology, its development and use, changes in political policies, dogmas and ideologies and changes in society in general all affect the way we do business, as we saw in the previous chapter.

For example, if there is economic recession this will affect consumer spending and consequently the demand for goods and services. If the government decides to deregulate certain activities in an industrial sector, then there will be a proliferation of companies entering that industry and the competition will become intense.

The nature of competition also affects the way businesses operate. Is your business competing with many other businesses? Is it competing nationally or internationally? Is it in a service or manufacturing sector? Is it in a regulated or deregulated industry?

All these questions affect the way you formulate your strategy. Strategy concerns the whole business interacting with its environment.

To compete effectively you have to adopt best practice in preparing your strategy. This involves focusing on the quality of your strategic thinking and looking at strategy in a holistic way, taking into consideration your resources and capabilities and matching them with your competitive environment.

> **KEY CONCEPT**
>
> To compete effectively you have to adopt best practice in preparing your strategy.

Organisations can achieve superior performance by taking advantage of opportunities available in the environment in which they do business and using or acquiring resources to transform them into capabilities.

The problem in practice is that as soon as one organisation gains a competitive advantage, that advantage disappears. To stop this happening, the capabilities created by an organisation have to be distinctive and they have to be difficult for competitors to copy.

> **KEY CONCEPT**
>
> The problem in practice is that as soon as one organisation gains a competitive advantage, that advantage disappears.

Best Practice in Preparing Your Strategy to Gain and Sustain Superior Performance

 ## BENCHMARKING

1 What business are you in?

Start by asking the question: What business are we in or do we want to be in? An ice-cream company wanting to dominate an existing market decided that it did not want to produce ice cream like its competitors but that it wanted to provide excitement and pleasure to a cross-section of segments in its particular market. This kind of thinking affected the way it manufactured its ice creams – they were very colourful, they had pleasant textures and both children and adults liked this type of ice cream compared to the boring, mono-colour and mono-textured ice cream produced by competitors.

Such a question also focused the company in terms of being innovative and different from its competitors.

2 Where are you now? Where do you want to go? How do you want to get there?

These questions will focus your attention on the content of your strategy, the processes you will need to adopt and the context within which your business operates.

These questions should also focus your attention on the direction you want to adopt. This is what strategy is all about. It is your pattern of decisions and activities that sets the long-term direction of your organisation.

Your strategy has to have a fit – a fit between the external environment and internal dimensions of your business. The next stage, therefore, is to analyse your external environment.

3 Analyse your external environment

Chapter 2 deals with the way organisations should conduct analysis of their external environment, taking into consideration the globalisation process.

4 Analyse your organisation internally

Look at the systems and the structure of your organisation. Can these respond to the strategy you want to or have adopted? Can they help you in delivering your strategy?

What are the skills and general quality of your staff? People should be your most important asset. Do they have the experience, skills and capacity to innovate in order to enable you to achieve your organisational goals? What type of leadership and culture exist in your organisation?

These are people-related and cultural issues (often referred as 'soft' issues) that constitute your organisational capabilities.

Resources and capabilities enable you to achieve superior performance. They form the business and the way you prepare and implement your strategy.

Resources and capabilities should be used to build a 'knowledge bank' in relation to innovating in your business and understanding and responding to the needs of your employees, customers and other partners with which you do business.

Your competitors can copy your systems and processes and thus erode your competitive advantage, but it is very difficult to copy what is in the heads of your staff. It is this that will give an organisation its distinctive capability. This is what is called 'tacit knowledge'. The conversion of this knowledge into explicit knowledge and its use will enable organisations to sustain and enhance superior performance.

5 Understand the importance of knowledge as a key organisational capability and use it to gain superior performance.

Knowledge is an appreciating asset. The more it is used, the more effective its application. In a modern context businesses have to come up with innovative structures and thinking in order to gain superior performance. Technology is there as an enabler, but the winning companies are those who learn to harness and use knowledge and become best practice leaders.

Knowledge must be distinguished from data and information. Many organisations believe that they are knowledge driven simply because they have a massive databank or they capture a range of information on their competition, competitors and customers.

The starting point, therefore, in striving to become a knowledge-driven organisation is to understand the nature of knowledge and knowledge management.

Data is raw material for information. It has no concept or meaning as such. When customers go to supermarkets to do their shopping, the shop has information on what is purchased when and how much money was spent. This is data, as it has no meaning or context.

When this information is put into context in terms of who made the purchase, whether the purchaser is a regular customer and why they shop at this particular shop, the data is transformed into information.

Information is organised and categorised data put into context. It has meaning and organisations can use it to create knowledge about their customers. For example, supermarkets can analyse information and get in touch with their regular customers to offer special promotions. They can take a variety of actions to retain their customers and build customer loyalty.

Knowledge is the *use* of information. If you can get your staff to use information

> **KEY CONCEPT**
>
> Knowledge is the *use* of information.

(including their training and experience), you have created knowledge. If this knowledge is codified or captured, you have created an appreciating, intangible asset for your organisation that, when used, will enhance your business performance.

 PAUSE FOR THOUGHT

The benefits of keeping staff informed of corporate developments are widely recognised. But when employees receive so much information that they begin to ignore it, there is a problem.

This is the situation that Clerical Medical was faced with recently. Process consultant Jayne Mitchell says staff felt they were drowning in information. She says, 'We used to get bulletins which ranged from "everybody must know this" to product information. Everything people wanted to communicate went onto the bulletin board, which was part of the e-mail system. You had to go in and look through it all to find what applied to you.'

Head of corporate affairs Tony Bloomer says the research revealed that staff felt they were bombarded with information that did not apply to them. The company opted for a complete redesign involving the staff newsletter, the intranet, internal television and team meeting procedure. (Witthaus, 2000)

Lessons to be learnt

- Information overload can stifle organisational communication.
- For information to be transformed into knowledge it has to be meaningful and relevant to the recipients.
- Information can be transformed into knowledge that then can be leveraged by the organisation if attention is paid to who and what information is to be provided.
- What Clerical Medical has done is an aspect of managing knowledge in its organisation.
- In practice we seem to drown in the ocean of data and die of thirst for relevant information at the same time.

Organisations have to learn to harness knowledge in order to compete effectively and improve their performance. A growing chunk of production in the modern economy is in the form of intangibles, based on the exploitation of ideas rather than material things. More and more goods, from Mercedes cars to Nike trainers, have increasing amounts of knowledge embedded in them.

> **KEY CONCEPT**
>
> Organisations have to learn to harness knowledge in order to compete effectively and improve their performance.

Knowledge comes in two formats. One is located in employees' heads, which is known as tacit knowledge, and the other is presented in written form and documents or embedded in products, and this is called explicit knowledge.

Some organisations have knowledge embedded in their processes and the knowledge there is between passive and explicit in format. The challenge for every organisation is to transform passive knowledge into active knowledge and to transform individual, tacit knowledge into group or team knowledge.

> **KEY CONCEPT**
>
> Managing knowledge is not rocket science – it is about creating an environment to encourage knowledge creation and transfer.

Organisations have to put processes in place and think of knowledge initiatives to bring about this transformation. Managing knowledge is not rocket science – it is about creating an environment to encourage knowledge creation and transfer.

Focusing on knowledge is not a fad; it has become a business necessity.

Why Are Organisations Reluctant to Manage Knowledge?

Feaful of investment

Many organisations believe that managing knowledge is about investing heavily in information technology and that they need to have specialists in the organisation to create and transfer knowledge.

This is not the case at all. Good leadership in any type and size of organisation can manage knowledge without spending heavily on IT. What is required is an understanding of what knowledge management is and what it involves.

You can spend thousands of pounds (and some organisations have done) and still not be able to manage knowledge and improve your performance. As the saying goes, *you do not lose weight by buying a better scale.*

Some feel that knowledge is not for business. It is intangible and as such it cannot be measured. If it is not measured it cannot be managed, they claim.

The modern economic system is increasingly based on knowledge. Organisations have constantly to innovate to improve their performance and to compete effectively. To do so is to take advantage of the wealth of experience, talent and skills in your organisation, because they constitute organisational knowledge.

Knowledge embedded in products and processes can be protected by law ithough copyright and patents and these can be managed and measured. To what extent employees create and transfer knowledge can be managed and measured as well.

In subsequent chapters we will examine the management and measurement factor.

Slow to adopt new thinking

Organisations are very slow to adopt new thinking. They feel they should let other organisations try the idea first and make mistakes and then they will follow.

As we saw earlier knowledge management is about as new as the Egyptian pyramids. However, due to accelerated changes in environmental factors and globalisation, organisations are operating in a complex environment. To respond

> **KEY CONCEPT**
> Knowledge management is as new as Egyptian pyramids.

effectively to such changes and to manage complexity requires good use of knowledge.

If you wait for other organisations to do this first, you will miss the boat and continually struggle to improve your performance.

Just managing information

Some organisations believe that they are managing knowledge when in fact they are simply managing information.

Managing knowledge involves focusing on employees, customers, partners, processes, motivation, culture and leadership. As we have seen in the case of Clerical Medical, providing information to all is not managing knowledge.

Three rings of change

Over the past few decades organisations have gone through three rings of change, namely reengineering, delayering and restructuring. In some cases their experiences have been traumatic and there were many human casualties. They do not want to jump through the hoop of knowledge management and re-experience the same kind of trauma.

Reengineering.

Michael Hammer and James Champy's book *Reengineering the Corporation* (1993) became a bestseller around the world as soon as it was published. People bought the book to find out the nature of business process reengineering and how it could help them improve their performance.

The book emphasised that change must be fundamental and radical, that the focus should be on process and that improvements must be dramatic. The idea was to analyse business processes and the various activities involved within each process and to eliminate activities that did not add value to business results, in particular results affecting customers.

There were many stories of organisations that embarked on business process reengineering. For example, some organisations achieved a fivefold reduction in cycle time as far as customer service was concerned. Some outperformed the industry in profitability. There were and are many success stories.

However, business process reengineering focused on processes and not on people. In this change initiative nothing was sacred. As one business executive put it, 'A company that has successfully been reengineered itself is like a phoenix rising from the ashes.'

Many organisations did not achieve the success they hoped for and, in spite of creating massive redundancies, the process had no impact on the bottom line.

It is instructive to look at some of the factors contributing to these failures so that such experiences are not repeated when it comes to organisations managing knowledge. Learning from past experiences creates new knowledge. Failures should be stepping stones towards success.

Consultancy firm McKinsey examined reengineering projects in more than 100 companies. The factors contributing to what appeared to be paradoxical outcomes included the following (*McKinsey Quarterly*, 1994):

- Redesign initiatives did not penetrate to the company's core and did not change roles and responsibilities, measurements and incentives, organisational structure, IT, shared values and skills.
- The process to be redesigned was not based on customer value.
- Senior executives did not invest enough time and energy.
- There was inadequate identification of the activities to include in the process being redesigned that were critical for value creation in the overall business unit.
- In some cases there was a lack of good leadership to lead the organisation through the period of change.
- There was resistance from key stakeholders.
- Not enough attention was paid to processes in those areas that fell short of customer expectations and competitive performance.

Note that these are very similar to the factors that have to be attended to by organisations that aspire to be knowledge driven.

In addition to these, other factors surfaced through various research studies. These were:

- Lack of resources.
- Cynicism and scepticism.
- Lack of skills and training.
- Poor teamwork.
- Lack of understanding of the nature of change.

Attention should be paid to these factors so that every organisation can benefit from a change initiative.

Delayering

Throughout history organisations have had to face up to a number of issues about the kind of structure that will best sustain the success of the business. For almost a century the most popular structure of the organisation was based on functional specialisation. Such a structure divides business into various compartments such as production, logistics, marketing and sales, finance and human resources.

Most organisations had a hierarchy with a very rigid structure and top-down communication flows. Within such a structure rules became depersonalised; specialisation and standardisation became the norm. What was needed was a structure that was flexible enough to respond to market changes and customer needs.

In the 1970s some organisations began to adopt a matrix structure in which projects were managed on a cross-functional basis and employees reported to a functional boss as well as a project leader. In many cases this structure created problems simply because it continued to function within the context of a hierarchical or pyramid structure.

In the 1980s management gurus advocated the adoption of a horizontal structure to respond to market needs. This was presented as the organisational structure of the twenty-first century.

Organisations decided to adopt this type of structure by reducing the number of layers of management, a practice known as delayering. Again, this created massive redundancies and the demise of 'middle-line' managers. Associated with this structure was the process of empowering the remaining employees.

For a long time employees were not sure 'who was next to go' and they also felt that their organisations wanted them to do more work with less resources.

Restructuring.

The third big ring of change was restructuring. Again, in the 1980s many organisations went through a process of downsizing and in some cases 'capsizing' to reduce costs. Initiatives involved changing the structure of the organisation and the roles and responsibilities of individuals. In some cases restructuring involved the relocation of the entire organisation.

Concurrently with restructuring, consultants were writing about the demise of long-term employment within an organisation. Employees were beginning to mistrust their companies.

Restructuring will continue as businesses merge and as downsizing becomes a fact of life. In some cases, however, the legacy is that survivors are scarred for a long time to come and lose their trust in management.

With these initiatives the focus was on information technology expenditure. The more information organisations gathered on the competitive environment and on their competitors, the better they thought they would become at competing effectively.

There was a great deal of confusion between information gathering and knowledge creation. Professor Charles West Churchman (1971) observed decades ago that 'knowledge resides in the user not in the collection of information … . It is how the user reacts to a collection of information that matters'.

In the light of the above experiences, many employees become nervous when you mention that managing knowledge is what should be done. This nervousness is understandable.

Managing knowledge should not involve radical changes within the organisation, however. It can be done at departmental level to start with and this best practice of managing knowledge can then spread throughout the organisation. So small organisations are ideally placed to manage knowledge.

> **KEY CONCEPT**
>
> Small organisations are ideally placed to manage knowledge.

 ## PAUSE FOR THOUGHT

A small printing company consists of three founding partners and four managers and they work with many associates and contract staff. The business has been in existence for 16 years and over this period the company felt there was no need to record experiences or project successes because the seven full-time members talked to each other regularly. There was therefore no necessity to build a knowledge bank.

Individual tacit knowledge was transferred to other members at an individual level. A year ago one of the founding partners who dealt with specific sector clients died of heart failure and one of the senior managers had to quit his job and left the country.

Suddenly the company felt that it could not perform properly as, with two longstanding members of the organisation leaving, its knowledge was 'walking out of the door'. It found it very difficult to conduct effective induction for two new recruits.

This company is now documenting its key processes and achievements at the end of each project and trying to capture and transform tacit knowledge into explicit knowledge in order to regain its superior performance.

In my experience it is precisely this type of organisation that needs to manage its knowledge. Whether you are large or small, for profit or not for profit, knowledge as an asset will deliver superior performance.

FOUR

Creating and Transferring Knowledge in Your Organisation: Focusing on Employees and Customers

Knowledge enables us to anticipate surprises and avoid landmines. (Anon)

Overview

- Organisations have to put processes in place to create and transfer knowledge.
- It is important to understand the nature of these processes.
- Various knowledge management initiatives are suggested to kick-start the processes.
- Communication is the core of knowledge creation and sharing.
- This chapter focuses on building a knowledge bank on employees and customers.

Tacit knowledge is transferred from one individual to another and from individuals to groups and teams through conversations, dialogues and meetings. Very often this transfer takes place informally, particularly at places like coffee machines.

A transfer from tacit to explicit knowledge takes place through the creation of documents, e-mails, reports and memos.

It is important to put processes in place to encourage knowledge transfer and knowledge sharing.

Benefits of Knowledge Transfer and Knowledge Sharing

- They stop you reinventing the wheel and as a result save time and reduce effort.
- They speed up decision-making processes.
- They provide an effective way of inducting new staff.
- They encourage the use of knowledge and promote collaboration.
- They capture knowledge for organisational use.
- They help trust become gradually institutionalised by collaborating and sharing.
- They encourage the transfer of best practice.
- They promote innovation in processes and products.
- They affect the bottom line – financial or otherwise.

Understanding the Process of Knowledge Transfer and Knowledge Sharing

Tacit knowledge is personal knowledge and in practice it is very difficult to communicate fully to others. It has a technical as well as a cognitive dimension. Explicit knowledge is the knowledge that has been articulated, coded and recorded.

> **KEY CONCEPT**
>
> Tacit knowledge is personal knowledge and in practice it is very difficult to communicate fully to others.

Two Japanese professors, Nonaka and Takeuchi (1995), presented a model of how organisations can create knowledge. Knowledge creation and transfer are achieved by interaction among individuals. In such interaction four modes of knowledge conversion take place: socialisation, externalisation, combination and internalisation.

Socialisation

Socialisation is a way of capturing an individual's tacit knowledge. It occurs by sharing experiences and on-the-job learning. Japanese companies often set up informal meetings outside the workplace where workers share their experiences of work-related projects and problems.

Nonaka and Takeuchi give the following example to explain this mode of knowledge creation. When Matsushita was developing an automatic bread-making machine in the late 1980s, its software engineers apprenticed themselves to the head baker of the Osaka International Hotel, who was reputed to produce the area's best bread, and discovered that the baker was not only stretching but also twisting the dough in a particular fashion, which turned out to be the secret for making tasty bread. Subsequently this practice was incorporated into the machine for making bread.

Externalisation

This is the process of converting tacit knowledge into explicit knowledge, taking the shapes of metaphors and analogies. At this stage tacit knowledge is transformed into models and hypotheses.

Nonaka and Takeuchi give examples of how Canon's mini-copier was created by such a process. One of the most difficult problems facing Canon was coming up with a low-cost, disposable cartridge that would eliminate the maintenance cost. One day, after consuming a few cans of beers, the group who were discussing this problem came up with the idea of examining beer cans and, after discussing similarities and differences, arrived at the technology to manufacture the aluminium drum at low cost. The disposable drum gave Canon a leadership position in the copier market.

Recently a television documentary showed how the tacit knowledge of heart surgeons has been programmed into robots, who are now capable of performing heart by-pass operations as long as a heart surgeon is in control of them.

Combination

This mode transforms explicit knowledge into further explicit knowledge by integrating different bodies of explicit knowledge.

Individuals discuss their explicit knowledge by phone, e-mail, meetings, seminars and documents.

When departments or teams decide to implement corporate objectives they take actions to achieve these objectives. This may involve conducting competitor analysis or environmental analysis or setting up performance appraisal systems.

For example, supermarkets may analyse their sales in terms of what products sell best, who buys them and in what quantities and they may through research and surveys find out the types of people who buy their products. Based on this information they can prepare promotion plans to increase sales.

Nonaka and Takeuchi give the example of Kraft General Foods, a manufacturer of dairy and processed foods, which uses data from retailers' POS (point-of-sale) systems to find out what sells and does not sell well, but also to create new ways of selling.

Internalisation

This is the process of transforming explicit knowledge into tacit knowledge. Individuals internalise their experiences. This mode is triggered off by 'learning by doing'.

Individuals perform certain tasks by reading manuals and documents. The authors give the example of GE, where all customer complaints are documented and a special database is prepared so that the new product development teams can read these complaints and 're-experience' for themselves what telephone operators encountered.

Internalisation can also happen if an individual is inspired by certain actions and emulates them.

Numerous organisations, such as Chevron, Dow Chemical, Skandia, Bankers Trust, Sun Microsystems and Ernst & Young to name but a few, have instituted these processes to create and transfer knowledge in their organisations.

Organisations do not have to use labels like 'socialisation', 'externalisation', 'combination' and 'internalisation'. They can create their own label. One organisation talks about communication, collaboration, organisation and learning, whereas, others simply talk about T-T, T-E, E-E, and E-T processes of knowledge creation.

What is important, however, is that processes have to be put in place to encourage knowledge creation and transfer and organisations also have to think about specific knowledge management initiatives under each process.

The following are examples of the knowledge management initiatives taken by some organisations.

- *Socialisation* – Brainstorming, informal meetings, discussions, dialogues, observation, on-the-job training, customer interaction, coaching, mentoring, learning groups.
- *Externalisation* – Meetings, building hypotheses and models, cartoons to communicate, after-action reviews, workshops, master classes, assignment databases, best practice exchange.
- *Combination* – Virtual library, publications, conferences.
- *Internalisation* – Facilitation skills, knowledge zone, client/customer feedback review, development counselling.

It is important to stress that the success of each mode of transformation will depend on the leadership and culture of organisation. After all, managing knowledge is all about creating a culture that will institutionalise trust and facilitate knowledge transfer and creation.

> **KEY CONCEPT**
>
> The success of each mode of transformation will depend on the leadership and culture of the organisation.

Most of these initiatives already exist in many organisations under the domain of management development. Using these initiatives to put the process of knowledge creation into processes, therefore, is not going to involve an organisation in massive investments in technology.

One of the key success factors for this process succeeding is communication within your organisation. Without effective communication, tacit knowledge remains tacit and organisations lose out.

> **KEY CONCEPT**
>
> Without effective communication, tacit knowledge remains tacit and organisations lose out.

Two aspects of communication should be paid attention to, communication within the organisation and interpersonal communication.

Communication within the organisation will be dealt with in Chapter 7 under corporate culture.

Interpersonal Communication

Interpersonal communication is communication between individuals. It involves understanding yourself and others. How do you communicate with your bosses and your colleagues?

- *Defensiveness* – In some cases we are very defensive in the way we communicate with our colleagues. We do not openly share our experiences. This could be due to a bad experience in the past or negative behaviour by our colleagues, or we may simply believe that 'knowledge is power' and not want to lose this power.
- *Shyness* – Some individuals are shy by nature and they do not like to 'boast' of their experiences. These are introverts who like to keep some information to themselves.
- *Hidden agendas* – In some organisations there are many 'hidden agendas' that form barriers to interpersonal communication.
- *Culture* – The culture of an organisation may not encourage open communication.

There are many barriers to interpersonal communication that must be addressed to facilitate knowledge flows.

Building Your Staff Knowledge

Making a start: understanding your employees and your customers

Any organisation, no matter how small, can make a start on managing knowledge by building the knowledge of its employees. There are three aspects of each employee's work-related experience and aspirations:

- *The job he/she is doing* – Current duties and responsibilities. Specific challenges and achievements in this job.
- *The job he/she can do* – This is over and above his/her current duties and responsibilities. This person can use his/her experience and training to do extra.
- *The job he/she would like to do* given the opportunity to acquire new or additional skills. This aspect covers the person's aspirations.

Gather information on these aspects as a starting point and you have the most valuable information on your staff that you can use (creation of knowledge) to develop your business and to achieve high performance.

This information should be documented and constantly updated. If acted on, such best practice can deliver the following results and behaviour:

- It will motivate your employees because they will feel you care about their aspirations.
- It will give you a clear understanding of what your employees perceive their current duties and responsibilities to be.
- It will give you an indication of how you can stretch your employees' capabilities.
- It will help you prepare an appropriate development plan for your employees.
- It will enable you to develop your business by identifying talent and knowledge that has remained tacit.
- It will promote a culture of open communication.
- It will motivate staff and help you institutionalise trust.
- It will enable you to benchmark against best practice and identify the gaps.
- It will give you a clear indication of the resources and capabilities of your organisation to compete effectively.

- It will enable you to assess the strategic fit of your organisation with what it aspires to achieve.

Recognising and measuring the efforts of your employees

This author, acting as management development coach, is surprised that many organisations still do not evaluate the performance of their staff properly. It was in 1960 that Douglas McGregor wrote:

> KEY CONCEPT
>
> This author, acting as management development coach, is surprised that many organisations still do not evaluate the performance of their staff properly.

Managers are uncomfortable when they are put in a position of playing God. The respect we hold for the inherent value of the individual leaves us distressed when we must take the responsibility for judging the personal worth of a fellow man.

Yet the conventional approach to performance appraisal forces us, not only to make such judgements and to see them acted upon, but also to communicate them to those we have judged. Small wonder we resist.

Best practice performance appraisal

It is important that your staff are actively involved in preparing their own performance objectives. This is an important aspect of motivating employees if you want to win their confidence and trust so that knowledge flows smoothly among individuals in your organisation.

> KEY CONCEPT
>
> It is important that your staff are actively involved in preparing their own performance objectives.

Ask staff to define their jobs (they are the best people to know what their jobs entail). Categorise activities involved in their jobs into key results areas or key performance areas (KRAs/KPAs). These are the outcomes you desire from them performing these activities. These areas could relate to operational, financial managerial, customer service, managing people and knowledge-sharing areas.

How should this be done in practice? Sit with your staff and go over the following:

My job is to do: ....

....

....

....

....

....

I perform the following tasks: ....

....

....

....

....

....

These tasks involve the following activities: ....

....

....

....

....

....

My objectives and desired outcomes are: ....

....

....

....

....

....

Having gathered this information, do make sure that your staff's objectives are aligned with overall corporate objectives.

In setting up the appraisal system, consider the following:

- What is expected from an individual.
- Why it is expected.
- How the outcomes are going to be measured.

- Who is going to measure them.
- What happens if there is under-performance.
- What are the rewards of over-achievement.

When the appraisal interview is arranged the manager or team leader should do his/her homework by getting full information on the individual concerned. The focus of the interview should be on analysing performance, not personality.

Feedback given when a person is not performing well should not be in a mode of 'negative feedback', which creates a barrier to communication. The feedback given should be constructive and specific. Feedback should address the following questions on behalf of those appraised:

- What is expected of me?
- How am I doing?
- Am I on target?
- How can I improve?
- Where can I get help?
- What is my reward?
- Where do I go from here?

In practice, those who conduct appraisal interviews face various kinds of problems: the measurement problem, the judgement problem, the organisation problem, the communication problem and the feedback problem.

The measurement problem arises due to ambiguity regarding the roles and responsibilities involved. In some cases the measures formulated are inappropriate and inadequate as not enough thought has gone into designing them. This is why it is important to clarify the duties and responsibilities involved.

The judgement problem occurs because many managers do not like to act as

> **KEY CONCEPT**
>
> Many managers do not like to act as a judge.

a judge. There are numerous cases in practice that show disagreements on ratings and their associated interpretations. Bias also creeps in when judgements are made on behaviour-based indicators.

The organisation problem is due to the fact that in some organisations staff appraisals are not taken very seriously. They are used as a window-dressing exercise. Some managers consider such appraisals as 'chores' and with such an attitude their hearts are not in evaluating their staff properly. This is perceived by the staff, who then lose faith in the system.

> **KEY CONCEPT**
>
> In some organisations staff appraisals are not taken very seriously.

The communication problem focuses on a lack of communication as to the purpose and importance of appraisals. Commitment and communication from top management are very important.

The feedback problem arises because many managers are not trained to give constructive feedback. This is why sometimes you hear staff say, 'He/she does not have a single nice thing to say about me and my performance.'

Performing appraisals properly leads to proper evaluation of the contribution made by your staff. If you want employees to trust you and share their tacit knowledge, you have create a climate of trust and communicate the message that people are indeed your greatest asset. You must convert hype into reality.

Focus on Customers

Peter Drucker, in his book *The Practice of Management* (1954), wrote:

> *If we want to know what a business is we must start with its purpose … there is only one valid definition of business purpose: to create a customer. What business thinks it produces is not of first importance – especially not to the future of the business or to its success. What the customer thinks he is buying, what he considers 'value' is decisive – it determines what a business is, what it produces, and whether it will prosper.*

This was written nearly 50 years ago and yet some organisations, big and small, are still struggling to deliver service excellence.

Building knowledge about your customers, therefore, is a must if you want to compete effectively and sustain your performance.

To become a customer-driven organisation, consider the following:

- What is your value proposition to your customers?
- Why do they do business with you?
- What is it that you do better or can do better than your competition that the customer perceives as valuable?
- Is it your product innovation or operational excellence or customer intimacy or a combination of all these that is significant?

Every business has to not just get close to its customers but consider its customers as partners. Customers are increasingly becoming more informed, more educated and more intelligent – they are creating their own *personal knowledge* to meet their needs effectively. They should be considered as value creators.

> **KEY CONCEPT**
>
> Every business has to not just get close to its customers but consider its customers as partners.

What can organisations do to listen to their customers?

- Establish customer focus groups and invite your customers to give you feedback on the way you deliver your products or services or to offer their views on product design.
- Visit your customers. Some organisations now take cross-functional groups to visit their customers to help them understand customer needs.
- Send questionnaires and conduct postal surveys to gather information on how customers perceive your organisation, your products and your services.
- Undertake customer care training to deliver excellent service.

The customer satisfaction aspects on which you need to build organisational knowledge should relate to the following:

- Determining customer requirements and expectations.
- The way you manage your relationship with your customers.
- What standards you have in place in relation to satisfying your customers.
- What complaint-resolution system you have established.
- Do you benchmark in order to adopt best practice?

Distribution company TNT, for example, in winning the European Quality award, focused its culture exclusively on anticipating and serving customers. Traditional transport businesses place a great emphasis on the hardware – depots, trucks, warehouses – and on shaping rosters. TNT, in contrast, resolutely styles itself as a service business, run by people to serve people. Although the company demonstrates innovative use of technology to solve complex problems, hardware is there solely to facilitate the job of satisfying customers and doing so more cost effectively than its competitors.

Many organisations pay lip service to delivering service excellence. They simply do not understand that building their customer knowledge is creating an intangible asset for their business and they can use this knowledge to win and keep customers.

> **KEY CONCEPT**
>
> Many organisations pay lip service to delivering service excellence.

You do not deliver excellence by simply appointing customer care staff or establishing a customer service department.

A certain furniture shop has a placard at its entrance proclaiming, 'Our purpose is to serve our customer'. A customer went into the shop with a view to spending about £15 000 to furnish her newly refurbished house. She chose a three-piece suite and some tables and chairs and, after making her decision, asked the assistant if the store would remove her old furniture. The assistant said it was not company policy to do so. The customer offered to pay up to £60 for this removal, but the assistant and the manager who was subsequently consulted refused. They lost that customer and £15 000 potential revenue.

Case Study: Striving to adopt best practice to support your customers – J D Edwards

J D Edwards is a $934m company based in Denver which provides integrated software for managing the enterprise and supply chain. J D Edwards' Customer Support Centre is based in High Wycombe.

How does a software system support call centre with more than 100 employees and a 'follow the sun', multi-lingual operation, deal with the problem of 26% of calls being misplaced in the call centre? By tearing up the most fundamental paradigm in call centre technology, the placement of agents into static groups defined by function or skill. In its place, it has implemented a design concept that creates the best possible group of resources for each caller – virtual groups on a call by call basis.

There's only two things you can do with a customer once they've bought your product – you can ignore them, or you can support them. Tempting as it is to pursue the former course – and there are, of course, companies that do opt for this business model – most companies simply can't get away with treating their customers like garbage. For them, customer support is vital.

'Customer support is one of the top mission critical functions for our company,' asserts Kevin Ramskir, EMEA Customer Support Technical Manager for enterprise software supplier, J D Edwards. 'It's our facing edge to our customers. Customer support has been the differentiator in swinging deals.'

But customer support faces two traditionally contradictory pressures – to be both cheap and good, efficient and effective. As anyone knows who has ever been told by a call centre computer that they are currently fourteenth in a queue and will be answered shortly, computerisation of customer support can be a two-edged sword. Whilst computer-aided call centres are the only practical means, in this mass market age, of interfacing to the customer base, the corporate support function has to

CONTINUED ... Case Study: Striving to adopt best practice to support your customers – J D Edwards

ensure that the way they operate works in favour of both the company and its customers.

This is just what J D Edwards hopes it has achieved with its new generation of call centre technology from Siemens. 'Our enterprise software products are the foundation on which companies build their businesses, and it is crucial that we have a market leading capacity to support them 24 hours a day, seven days a week,' says Ramskir.

The bottom line of customer support is recognising that customers do not want to need it – nobody wants to have problems. It's a phone call nobody wants to make. So when a customer does pick up the phone to customer support he wants the experience to waste as little time as possible, and solve his problem as fast as possible. Some customer problems, says Ramskir, can be solved by reference to the company's web site.

'We have a very extensive knowledge garden on the web containing all sorts of information – the site can track calls, looking for keywords in association with the customer's problem, and download code fixes,' says Ramskir. 'We encourage customer self service, but we give them the choice of dealing with us direct.'

Given the highly complex product set J D Edwards supplies to run major enterprises, it's not surprising that sometimes only a live brain will do – in which case the customer wants to reach it as quickly as he can. 'The volume of calls is not high – we get around seven thousand calls a month rather than seven thousand a day – but the queries are complex because of the complexity in the software,' says Ramskir.

There are also peaks and troughs, notably those tracking the accounting year. 'The end of the month, quarter, half or full

CONTINUED ... Case Study: Striving to adopt best practice to support your customers – J D Edwards

financial year can be periods of very high anxiety for our customers,' says Ramskir. 'They have to produce very large business reports and hammer the software.'

Anything that may prevent them doing so elicits an immediate call to customer service at J D Edwards – and a request for an immediate answer to complex software. That means that a customer has to be put in touch with the right expert for his problem. The first key task, therefore, is to identify the problem, and pass the caller to the consultant with the answer.

Based in High Wycombe, J D Edwards' Customer Support Centre looks after the company's thousand-plus customers throughout Europe, the Middle East and Africa, as well as J D Edwards' business partners and its own field consultants. 'We're the single point of contact for all J D Edwards' post-implementation issues,' says Ramskir.

As an international support centre with over a hundred staff, 'We support six languages – French, Italian, Spanish, German, Dutch and English – which is unusual in the industry,' he points out. Between sixty and seventy percent of the calls are in English, although the support centre has consultants who are native speakers in all languages on site.

Up until the summer of last year the company had, says Ramskir, 'a fairly aged, green screen call-tracking system, about half a dozen years old, which required an administration team to handle the customer calls. They would take a call centre customer details, verify them, get a brief description of the problem and identify the product range, and make the best efforts to place the call in a queue so that any one of a set of consultants could pick it up and take the call. It was a fairly typical human intervention model.' What was wrong with it? 'The administrator had to decide where to place the call – and

CONTINUED ... Case Study: Striving to adopt best practice to support your customers – J D Edwards

not spend too much time about it!' says Ramskir. 'That was high pressure.'

Inevitably, there was a degree of both inaccurate entry of details which meant that the consultant would sometimes need to re-enter them correctly, and an inability to find the best expert for the problem. Metrics showed that over a quarter, 26%, of calls were being misplaced in the call centre. 'There was a very strong possibility that we couldn't find the person with the right skills (for the problem), and had to get them to call back the customer,' recalls Ramskir.

This was aggravating, and not just for the customer. It wasted J D Edwards' time as well. Having, as Ramskir points out, 'very high level support people – I've been in customer support for over twenty years and I've never seen a higher quality set of people, including qualified accountants and a high proportion with university degrees,' it was frustrating that customers with a problem couldn't get through faster to an expert with an answer.

But around two years ago the company went to Siemens to find a better solution. Siemens came up with two products – Interactive Voice Response (IVR) and Resume Routing. The two products work in tandem. IVR identifies the customer and his problem, Resume Routing identifies the consultant who can deal with it and puts the customer on to him. But identifying the call type and building the customers' call profile is non-trivial.

'We can have a hundred different call types,' says Ramskir. Add in the six languages the centre supports, 'makes a combination of 600,' he says. That's high for the call centre industry. One mobile phone company, recalls Ramskir, thought they had a complex set up with twelve call types – 'though they were high volume,' he concedes.

CONTINUED . . . Case Study: Striving to adopt best practice to support your customers – J D Edwards

Customer calls also have to be matched against the level of service they have opted for. 'We have three support levels,' says Ramskir. 'The standard is where they can call their local support centre – us – during office hours. Next is where they can call us seven by twenty four, and the third is where we provide a special, fixed-price 48-hour weekend service when customers are doing an upgrade.' As it seeks out the best person to solve the problem in the incoming call type, RR can recognise when an appropriate agent is already engaged, and will widen its search for the next best while continuing to try the first choice agent in case he comes off the phone. Once the call has been placed, the virtual group is disbanded.

'True skills-based call management provides a significantly enhanced solution for maintaining a unique skill set for each and every consultant,' says Ramskir. 'For example, the consultant may speak multiple languages, know J D Edwards OneWorld finance applications, and have specific in-depth skills in accounts payable and a good awareness of receivables. With RR each of these skill areas and the skill level can be populated in the telephone system and weighted with appropriate preferences.'

If an agent handling a call gets stuck, he can escalate it to a more senior consultant. Ultimately, problems can be referred back to J D Edwards' development centre in Denver.

Once the call is in the system, the queuing mechanism of RR is used to relax requirements automatically in response to undue customer waiting times. This expands the pool of resources available to serve the customer without management intervention. If no agent becomes available after a set period of time the call is channelled back to a member of the administrative team.

CONTINUED ... Case Study: Striving to adopt best practice to support your customers – J D Edwards

Before the new system went live, J D Edwards sent out notification to all customers, starting with a letter, including an information pack and a prompt card in local language. 'We sent out cards to customers translated into every language,' says Ramskir. This, ironically, proved a considerable challenge. 'When it came to Dutch we couldn't quite translate the sense of what we wanted to say – we spent three weeks trying and gave up!'

The company also had to be aware of nuances of meaning in foreign languages – the Italians interpreted a reference to the J D Edwards sales production module as the company's intention of wanting to sell them something. 'The biggest challenge was getting the translation done,' recalls Ramskir. 'You can blunder and offend if you're not careful.'

Adopting the new technology has also enabled J D Edwards to make more use of its customer support consultants as they come on stream. RR allows managers to gradually increase the exposure of employees as they become more experienced and better trained.

'The learning curve is sometimes three to six months before we can place an agent comfortably on to the phones,' says Colin Balmforth. 'With RR we can now deploy an agent within one week because their skill set can be tightly controlled and they will not receive calls outside their knowledge area.'

The new system also contains in-built reporting tools which provide crucial feedback as to how customers are behaving and how available agents are, gathering metrics on such things as customer call abandonment rate – giving up in despair – agent availability, length of call and time to resolution. Metrics is an area that Ramskir wants to expand. 'The reporting side (of RR) is not a massive strength – we want more sophisticated call

---

CONTINUED ... Case Study: Striving to adopt best practice to support your customers – J D Edwards

reporting, for example to understand *why* customers abandon calls," he says.

The overall direction for the centre's new technology generation is, says Ramskir, 'very much towards full customer relationship management. At the moment we're still using a proprietary system developed in house which is nowhere near enough – we're working with Siemens now on this and expect to have it in place in the autumn.'

Eventually, with comprehensive, deep understanding of customer behaviour when calling the support centre, J D Edwards, says Ramskir, will be in a good position to complete a virtuous circle, feeding back the centre's findings to each customer's account manager in order to throw up any gaps, say, in areas such as initial customer training.

With a corporate strategy of turning customer support from a cost base to a revenue earner, one thing, argues Ramskir, is definite. Has the new generation call centre technology earned its keep and won return on investment? 'Yes,' says Ramskir. 'We now have a leading edge, award winning call centre to support our customers.'

Reproduced by permission of Reed Publishing and the BuyIT Best Practice Group. First published in the *BuyIT Best Practice* series in *Computer Weekly* magazine, 2001.

Satisfying your customers and satisfying your employees should go hand in hand. Building a knowledge bank on your employees' skills, experience and aspirations and on your customers' buying habits, need and expectations is the best

> **KEY CONCEPT**
>
> Satisfying your customers and satisfying your employees should go hand in hand.

practice you could adopt to become a knowledge-driven organisation.

FIVE

Technology and Knowledge Management

Don't just learn the tricks of the trade, learn the trade. (Anon)

Overview

- The diffusion of technologies has enabled the capturing of complicated information and the creation of knowledge.
- The Internet has been the most effective catalyst in knowledge creation.
- E-businesses are configuring the way business is conducted today.
- The CBI's survey *The Quiet Revolution* has highlighted the key developments taking place in e-businesses in the UK.
- The Internet has been one of the most significant tools for sharing and transferring knowledge.
- Organisations have to make sense of the information captured and transform that information through a 'sense-making process' into useful knowledge.
- Three case examples are given to show how SMEs have used technologies to connect people with people and people with technologies.

Over the past decade there has been a diffusion and convergence of technologies that has facilitated quantum leap developments in managing information. Advances in technology are taking place at a breathtaking pace. Markets are being transformed by the effects of cyberspace.

Everyone is familiar with the Internet and yet a decade ago it was unthinkable that an international network could grow to millions of users in a very short period. New technologies and their falling costs have become the important catalysts in changing the way business is being conducted. One must also not forget that the faster rate of breakthroughs makes organisational uniqueness and distinctive capabilities obsolete very fast.

> **KEY CONCEPT**
>
> Over the past decade there has been a diffusion and convergence of technologies that has facilitated quantum leap developments in managing information.

> **KEY CONCEPT**
>
> New technologies and their falling costs have become the important catalysts in changing the way business is being conducted.

 PAUSE FOR THOUGHT

- A third of US companies will bill online by 2004.
- The Chinese Internet population is approaching 23 million.
- 20% of the Portuguese population is online.
- The Austrian Internet audience is 2.7 million.
- 11% of British current account holders are banking online.
- In its latest eEurope Report, e-Marketer predicts that the number of Internet users will grow from 70 million at the end of 2000 to 108 million by end of 2001 and 255 million by 2004.
- Customers who buy more often and spend more money online are most likely to shop at web sites that offer personalisation.
- UK employers are largely happy with online recruitment services and may plan to increase their budgets for spending with these sites, according to Forrester.

The Internet

The Internet consists of a variety of components, e.g. e-mail, text documentation, databases, discussion groups, newsgroups, real-time chat, video and audio conferencing.

The Internet is a tool and its biggest impact is speed. It delivers speed of deliberation, transactions and information.

Countries that have advanced telecommunications infrastructures are likely to have faster and more reliable Internet access.

Many organisations believe that managing knowledge involves heavy expenditure on IT and employing specialists in knowledge management. This is not the case. Technology is an enabler. Vendors of knowledge management systems are in fact selling software to facilitate the storage, transfer and management of information.

Managing knowledge is about managing your people to use information on customers, products, processes and partners to create knowledge for the organisation. To become a knowledge-driven organisation requires a new way of thinking and

> **KEY CONCEPT**
>
> Managing knowledge is about managing your people to use information on customers, products, processes and partners to create knowledge for the organisation.

a new mindset that crosses all boundaries between profit and not-for-profit organisations and between different sizes of organisation.

Technology has enabled many organisations to capture and manage such information.

What are the capabilities of the Internet?

- It facilitates the spread of information.
- It creates a market where buyers and sellers can come together.
- It facilitates human interaction, thus enabling the transfer of information and the creation of knowledge.
- It does not discriminate between global companies and SMEs.
- It enables companies to reinvent themselves.
- It offers significant market opportunities to start-ups.
- It is being used to manage inventory very effectively.
- It enables organisational resources and capabilities to be stretched strategically.
- It gives consumers pricing information.
- It slashes time and costs out of the supply chain. It triggers innovation in software, communication technologies and the way organisations deal with suppliers, manufacturers and customers.

- It provides global reach in marketing.
- It enables organisations to source talent and people to source information on organisations.
- It facilitates networking and effective knowledge creation.
- It enables one-to-one marketing.

Building a web site

If you are going to build a web site for your organisation, consider the following:

- Is it fast and user-friendly?
- Does it add value for your customers?
- Is information updated regularly?
- Does it incorporate adequate customer support?
- Is it too complicated?

Intranets and extranets

An intranet is a technological infrastructure employing Internet open systems standards and protocols to implement a corporate network. Organisations use intranets to distribute information and data at high speed among their offices.

Intranet activities usually take place behind secure 'firewalls' so that only authorised users have access. An intranet is a very effective tool for managing knowledge within the organisation.

Organisations use intranets to:

- Provide daily briefings to their staff.
- Operate a project management database.
- Give information on policies and procedures.
- Monitor orders from customers.

When the company makes its internal network or intranet accessible to its partners, the intranet becomes an extranet.

The Impact of E-business

The CBI Survey *The Quiet Revolution* (CBI/KPMG, 2001) highlights the following in relation to the development of e-business in the UK:

76 per cent of companies currently generate less than 5 per cent of their turn over from e-business. But this trend is to change dramatically with 58 per cent expecting to derive at least 10 per cent of their revenue directly from e-business within the next two to three years.

Many businesses are now using the internet to transform their businesses into click-and-mortar and in some cases purely click businesses.

> **KEY CONCEPT**
>
> Many businesses are now using the internet to transform their businesses into click-and-mortar and in some cases purely click businesses.

40 per cent of firms are finding that e-business is already having a real impact on all aspects of the organisation with only 17 per cent reporting a limited impact.

90 per cent expect e-business to have some impact in the next two to three years.

The rise and fall of the dotcoms may have dominated the first wave but the second is now being led by traditional organisations across the UK of all sizes in every sector, with all companies expected to step up their e-business activity over the next two to three years.

According to the *Economist*, some bosses in traditionally technology-resistant industries may still think that the Internet is nothing to do with them, but their numbers are dwindling fast.

Using the Internet in Knowledge Management

The Internet can facilitate the performance of various key activities necessary for knowledge creation and knowledge transfer and sharing. These activities are:

- Capturing data and information.
- Mapping networks of experts.
- Sharing knowledge and best practice.
- Recording experience.
- Embedding knowledge in products, processes and people.

> **KEY CONCEPT**
>
> The Internet can facilitate the performance of various key activities necessary for knowledge creation and knowledge transfer and sharing.

There are many knowledge tools available in the market place such as video conferencing, groupware, electronic data interchange, shared databases and other knowledge-based systems. Here we focus attention on the Internet as an enabler of knowledge creation and transfer.

The Internet is very valuable for obtaining information from various experts and for conducting searches. Internet functions such as FTP (file transfer protocol) and the World Wide Web (WWW) provide easy access to information, which can also be obtained via discussion groups and news groups.

The Internet can also give access to published information on various companies and industrial sectors.

Furthermore, it plays a significant role in facilitating customer interaction. It enables a business to capture valuable data that can then be structured in a meaningful way to create business information on its customers. A one-to-one relationship can be created by sending regular e-mails on the status of orders and providing information on other products.

Surveys can be done via the Internet and the organisation can analyse responses and build a good bank of customer information.

> **KEY CONCEPT**
>
> To make sense of the ocean of information you need to go through a sense-making process.

To make sense of the ocean of information you need to go through a sense-making process. This involves five key sub-processes: information gathering, analysis, synthesis, sharing and reuse.

BENCHMARKING

Information gathering

- Gather information on who does what, how and where. Identify the key players and the experts related to the projects you plan to undertake.
- Contact people to 'pick their brains'. Mine as much tacit knowledge as you can.
- Record all the information.

Analysis

- Find out what you have and how you are going to categorise the information you have collected.
- Categorise information according to your project needs.
- Analyse information by looking at the kind of information you have and its significance.
- Consider if you need to do any follow-up work.

Synthesis

- Determine the outcomes of your analysis.
- Record the outcomes.
- Sharing
- Share the information among project members.

Reuse

- Do not reinvent the wheel. Reuse the information you have recorded. This is how information is transformed into organisational knowledge.

Technology and Knowledge Creation

Below are some real-life cases showing how companies are using digital technology to adopt best practice operations to enhance their business performance.

Case Study: Technology in training – Knowledge=Power Ltd

Virtual reality and digital networks are saving companies up to 50% of their training budgets in reduced travel and subsistence costs and increased opportunity time for those who would otherwise be away from their workplace.

Call centres are among the early adopters: first among the efficient new industries to use virtual learning is the telephone sales and service sector. It is one of the fastest growing sectors in UK business (over 40% in 1998, source Call Centre Association) and Knowledge=Power Ltd's own interactive learning course selected for Millennium Product recognition is already regarded as one of the best of the new breed of multimedia training. With the Virtual Learning Centre™, all the learning takes place in Knowledge=Power's Virtual Learning Centre. This is a virtual reality building which contains a classroom, and a library where study takes place and games and exam rooms where students then test their knowledge. The Communication Room gives access to the Internet or company intranet. Navigation around the six rooms is done with single clicks of the mouse to activate familiar objects such as a slide projector, VCR and books in the library.

Telephone Sales – a personal development programme, designed to teach all levels of people the principles and best practices of opening, controlling and closing a sales call – this 6 hour course introduces the core skills of active listening, needs identification, communication of benefits, empathy and objection-handling for all those using the phone for their living.

Kevin Gavaghan, Managing Director of Knowledge=Power Ltd, talks about the innovation process behind the development of the Telephone Sales Personal Skills programme:

'Market research showed the huge pent-up demand for training of this type. Staff recruitment and staff turnover in the call centre industry and businesses with large branch/sale networks are at least 20% p.a. and the number of skilled classroom trainers is limited. The close match between customers' researched needs and the quality and focus of the finished product. From conception to launch took twenty-six weeks, the product was launched at the back end of 1997.'

From the original research, the company was able to build a well-priced training product that met the specified need. The communications programme was carefully targeted in advance and carried out by experienced sales teams.

Sales are in line with expectations and Knowledge=Power Ltd is evaluating the product's performance through customer satisfaction research.

The company is keen to develop new products and has an in-house design team, systems in place for the regular generation of ideas and innovation and also a documented process for new product development, which was used for this particular product. Indeed, over the past five years, over ten percent of the company's output has been new and innovative.

Taken from the CBI's *Fit for the Future* web site: www.fitforthefuture.co.uk
Reproduced by permission of the CBI.

Lessons learnt

- How technology can be used to reduce costs.
- How technology can create learning zones.
- How technology can provide 'continuous' training.
- There is no need to send people outside for training.
- Technology can enable the adoption of best practice.
- Technology can overcome a shortage of skilled staff.

Case Study: How technology can link internal and external dimensions of business – Scotch Whisky Association

The Scotch Whisky Association, based in Edinburgh, wanted to improve the way it operated, both internally within its own office and externally within the Scotch whisky industry. It has managed to achieve its objectives by harnessing the business benefits of information and communication technology.

Internally the Association now uses a networked computer system for accounting and for designing and producing its own publications. It also has a digital telephone system and a digital online photocopier and printer. This has allowed them to work more efficiently, automating processes that previously had to be done manually. Networking information means that it can be easily found and duplication is avoided.

Externally it has created a Scotch whisky website for the public and an extranet so it can communicate electronically with members. It is encouraging members to use e-mail and the Internet. E-mailing information and committee papers to its members is simple and fast. Research is easier as more and more EU and government industry legislation and data is now available, free, on the Internet. The Association now links members who may require further information directly to the appropriate EU or government website.

Its own website has improved public awareness. Scotch whisky is sold all over the world and the website allows it to market the product, cheaply, to a global audience.

The Association is increasingly seen by its members as pro-gressive and proactive. Future plans include allowing members to use the website to order publications, obtain industry statistics, and access an interactive Tax and Duties database for all countries to which Scotch whisky is exported.

Before implementing technology solutions, Director of Finance Jim Devin gives this advice:

CONTINUED ... Case Study: How technology can link internal and external dimensions of business – Scotch Whisky Association

'Know exactly what you are trying to achieve but stay flexible for any unscheduled developments as the projects start to take shape. If the right professional advice is used, all will be well.'

Taken from the CBI's *Fit for the Future* web site: www.fitforthefuture.co.uk Crown Copyright material is reproduced with the permission of the Controller of HMSO and the Queen's printer for Scotland.

Lessons learnt

- Decide exactly what it is you want to achieve.
- How technology can be used to improve operational performance.
- How technology can be used to network.
- Technology enables the sharing of information.

Case Study: Technology and people involvement – NatWest Life

How does an insurance company introduce a new system that will deliver a step change in productivity (target 50% improvement) in less than two months, without alienating its staff? The solution is to bring in an image and workflow system and integrate it with existing systems with the close cooperation of both technology partners and key business users, working to a detailed change and benefit management plan.

That's what NatWest Life & Regulated Sales, the life and pensions business of NatWest bank, did. And they successfully achieved a 50% improvement in productivity. There can't be many industries where the back office is more traditionally paper-based than in the insurance business. So if any sector is ripe for workflow automation it's in such an environment.

But IT investments require pay back. That meant setting an extremely high target to achieve. Instead of being content with the standard 20–30% productivity gain, the project had to enable clerical end-users to do half as much work again as they normally did. Nick Thomas, Head of Product Services at NatWest Life and Regulated Sales, and Project Manager says: 'There was no way we'd have done the project if we hadn't aimed to get a 50% improvement. The financial case was very marginal, and we set the payback period for three to four years. If we'd said we wanted payback within say 12 months we'd not have gone forward.'

What complicated the return on investment equation was a factor that nearly every organisation encounters when making technology-led investments – the bigger picture.

For NatWest Life, the bigger picture was framed by the fact that the bank's life assurance business was set up in 1993, and to get to market fast, the company took existing life assurance IT systems from another company. This meant that it could start selling policies fast, but the trade-off was this also meant it had bought itself an instant legacy system.

'There's been various attempts to migrate us away since then, but to replace all the back office systems would mean looking at spending over £20m,' says Thomas.

The design phase, divided into two, business and technical, took five months until November that year, although building got going in October and was complete by March 1998. Testing ran from March to June, and then a phased implementation began, with the first phase complete by the end of June, and the last complete by August. When rolled out, users got the full functionality of the system in one go.

'Everything had to be there from day one,' says Thomas. 'It was big bang in terms of functionality, but with a slow (phased) turn on.'

Right from the start NatWest Life took care to ensure that 'business involvement' did not just mean involvement at the level of managers. The system's end-users, whose way of

CONTINUED ... Case Study: Technology and people involvement – NatWest Life

working would be significantly changed by implementing workflow, were closely involved too.

'We identified one person in each end-user team of around 25 staff to be the team's representative,' says Thomas. Each team rep was then 'on attachment' to the project and was trained up on the new systems, heavily involved in system and user acceptance testing, and in drawing up the intensive three day training the rest of their teams would go through.

NatWest Life also ensured that any lack of mental buy-in to the project by operations managers whose business processes were being work-flowed was avoided by changing their budgets in line with the project's expected effects on productivity.

'From the moment we said we'd do the project, all the operational budgets for the areas to be impacted were changed in line with the benefits,' says Thomas.

It was therefore up to the operational managers to ensure that cooperation with the new system enabled the benefits to be harvested, or else, says Thomas, 'they'd be looking at cost overruns on their own budgets.'

There was also a significant degree of change management involved. The way that end-users worked would be changed and they had to be prepared for that, rather than discovering it once the system had been rolled out.

'We'd expected it to take until six months after implementation to get back to the level playing field (pre-project work throughput) but we experienced nothing like that. Within about a month of rolling the system out we were level again, and had achieved our (productivity improvement) targets by November,' says Thomas.

Since then, the workflow system has been continuously improved to implement corresponding improvements in the design of the underlying process, in order to make them ever

> **CONTINUED ... Case Study: Technology and people involvement – NatWest Life**
>
> more efficient and faster to execute. There has also been a follow-on in terms of change management, in order to defuse fears of deskilling amongst the end-user workforce now that so much of their job has been computerised, with the system pulling through the processes automatically. In response, jobs have been re-enskilled.
>
> The final benefit is perhaps less tangible, but no less valuable. 'Part of the integration contract with Unisys, was that NatWest Life wanted a good representation of its own IT people on the Unisys team. The result is that NatWest Life now has its own experienced experts at designing, building, integrating and implementing an image and workflow system.'
>
> Reproduced by permission of Reed Publishing and the BuyIT Best Practice Group. First published in the *BuyIT Best Practice* series in *Computer Weekly* magazine, 2001.

Lessons learnt

- Balance technological needs with people needs.
- Use technology to increase efficiency.
- Involve staff in planning.
- Plan adequately.
- Continuously monitor progress.

Customers and Technology: Creating Customer Knowledge

Relationship marketing calls for customer-oriented production and delivery of services and products, be it by click or mortar organisations. Database technology enables companies to gather a vast amount of information on individual customers and their needs and preferences. Companies that create relationships with customers will be able to retain them for a very long time.

According to Fredrick Reichheld of Bain & Co, raising customer retention rates by five percentage points increases the value of the average customer by 25–100%. The retained customer also costs less to service than the cost of acquiring new customers, although winning new customers is important as well.

Relationship marketing:

- Focuses on customers.
- Is concerned with customer retention.
- Focuses on customer value.
- Puts high emphasis on delivering excellence.
- Sees quality as the concern of all staff.

For relationship marketing to succeed organisations must have:

- Capacity to deliver.
- Information on their customers.
- Staff who understand the value of relationships with their customers.

To gain and retain customers, the four 'P's of marketing (price, place, promotion and product) have to be replaced by four 'C's – customer, communication, conviction and commitment.

A note of caution

In relationship marketing, it is also very important to note that technology must not alienate customers.

Furber (2000) makes the point that many companies are neglecting their customers. Those that depend heavily on technology and fail to combine it with human contact will find themselves losing clients quickly.

> **KEY CONCEPT**
>
> In relationship marketing, it is also very important to note that technology must not alienate customers.

Many marketers work on the premise that consistent communication with the consumer is an essential part of successful customer relationship management (CRM).

For this to happen, technology needs to play a major role. However, an over-reliance on technology means companies can neglect the basic principles of marketing – the winning of customers through great ideas and creativity.

But getting the right mix between technology and marketing is a delicate balancing act as Clive Mcnamara, marketing director of CRM solution provider AIT Group, reveals.

He cites the example of a company AIT worked for last year called M Finance – the first online mortgage broker in the UK – which was too technology-led. He says, 'It was launched with only 30 people so it was incredibly automated. But it didn't get the marketing right. Nobody had heard of it so it rapidly went out of business. You can do a hell of a technology job, but if you don't do the right marketing job you'll end up going to the wall.

'A problem for CRM is that the whole concept appears to have been caught up in the hype surrounding new channels to market, and the headlong rush to deliver a consistent message across all communication platforms. In their haste, companies tend to focus heavily on technology, and end up forgetting about the customer.

'With many companies now, when you call them you have about five options to go through before you even speak to a human voice. Technology can end up putting distance between the company and its customers.'

SIX

The Leadership Factor and Knowledge Management

As I grow older, I pay less attention to what men say, I just watch what they do. (Andrew Carnegie).

Overview

- Managing knowledge is about creating the right environment within your organisation.
- Effective leadership is also about creating the right environment.
- Two case examples are given showing how SMEs can create an appropriate organisational climate.
- Modern leaders are faced with the challenges of globalisation and galloping technology.
- Such challenges demand innovative responses. They require leaders to transform their organisations and empower their staff.
- Empowering staff facilitates decision making close to the customer.

Managing knowledge is about creating an organisational environment that leads to the creation and sharing of knowledge within the organisation. This is one of the key attributes of effective leadership.

Leadership is a process of influencing individuals and guiding others towards

KEY CONCEPT

Managing knowledge is about creating an organisational environment that leads to the creation and sharing of knowledge within the organisation.

desired goals. Over the years various theories of leadership have been put forward by management writers. Most of these theories originating in the US can be categorised into:

- Trait theories.
- Behavioural theories.
- Situational theories.

Trait theorists believe that leaders are born, not made. Great leaders have inherent traits such as high intelligence, understanding of people, self-confidence and charisma. According to this school of thought, leadership is a cluster of outstanding qualities inside the leader.

Behavioural theorists see leadership behaviour as existing on a continuum ranging from authoritarian behaviour at one end to a participative style at the other. Researchers identified two major behaviours called consideration – relating to a focus on people – and initiating structure – relating to a concern for the task.

Situational theorists emphasise the role of situational factors. The appropriate style of leadership is a function of:

- Leader–follower relationship.
- Task structure.
- Position power. Telling, selling, participating and delegating depend on the readiness of the group to take responsibility.

Effective leadership relates to the style adopted depending on situational factors. The best leaders are those who adapt their styles according to various types of people and situations.

These various theories and their associated training courses identify and emphasise only some aspects of leadership, the focus being on the style one adopts.

Leadership and the Pygmalion Effect

Professor J. Sterling of Harvard University asserted that leaders who have confidence in their ability to develop and stimulate followers to higher levels of performance will treat them with confidence and self-esteem. Such leaders exert a positive influence and obtain better results.

According to Jack Welch, former CEO of General Electric,

Good business leaders create vision, articulate the vision, passionately own the vision, and relentlessly drive it to completion. Above all else, though good leaders are open. They go up and down, and around their organisation to reach people. They don't stick to the established channels. They are informal. They are straight with people. They make a religion out of being accessible.

> **KEY CONCEPT**
>
> Good business leaders create vision, passionately own the vision, and relentlessly drive it to completion.

The need for effective leadership applies to every type of organisation. Usually researchers and books focus on big businesses and their leaders. The following are two cases from very small but successful businesses.

Case Study: Simon Jersey Ltd

Simon Jersey Ltd in Accrington hosts bespoke visits as part of the best practice Inside UK Enterprise scheme (IUKE). This leading designer and supplier of corporate clothing joined the Department of Trade and Industry funded scheme this year and has already won its highly coveted Best New Host Award.

President of Simon Jersey, Simon Moyle, greets the visitors and explains the ethos of the company that he has built up over the last 30 years. Thanks to his strong vision 'to be the best in the industry', Simon Jersey has grown from a small shop on the cobbled streets of Accrington, to the specially designed high-tech headquarters for the 300-strong team on the outskirts of the town.

CONTINUED ... Case Study: Simon Jersey Ltd

Technical Director Richard Mullen then explains how in the past ten years, sales have quadrupled from £7 million to £28 million and the exclusive range of corporate wear is now selling in 120 countries worldwide, with over 66,000 customers in the UK. He emphasised that the key to success is hard work and the strong enthusiastic culture that has developed within Simon Jersey of enjoying yourself when you come to work.

Following a tour of the headquarters, discussions with shop floor and sales staff, and a networking lunch, Richard continues the presentation on inspiring people to succeed and promoting change: 'Good communication is essential. We ensure everyone is clear on how our business is doing against objectives. After the director's and manager's monthly meetings, information is cascaded throughout the business within a matter of hours.'

'We've also set up a Care Team across the departments and value their suggestions on improvements and efficiencies. A money saving scheme set up asking all employees for an idea, achieved a cost saving of approximately £400,000 and more than paid for a Dale Carnegie leadership training programme.'

He concluded: 'Everyone has the ability to inspire others, but not everyone uses it. Make a difference today.'

A broad spectrum of companies from Scotland, England and Wales are represented at these one-day networking event. These have included the Operations Director of Lyle and Scott in Hawick, the MD of Bees Knees Day Nursery in Bridgend and the Managing Director of Excel Electronic Assemblies in Wales.

Both Tom Sellar and Jan Robson, Operations and Personnel Directors of Lyle and Scott in Hawick, found the day very useful and informative. Jan explained: 'This is the first IUKE visit we have been on and think it's excellent value for money. Even within the first hour we had so much useful information that it had been worth the journey and day out of the business.' Tom

CONTINUED ... Case Study: Simon Jersey Ltd

added: 'Probably the most value for me was seeing the type of environment in which people can excel.'

Debbie Gray, Training Officer at HM Customs and Excise, travelled over 500 miles to attend and is convinced of the value of the scheme. 'I've encouraged at least 20 people from my organisation to take part in the visits and they've all come back full of new ideas and highly motivated. We've even set up coffee mornings to promote IUKE to the other 500 employees in our division to explain the benefits.'

MD from Mettler Toledo, supplier of precision weighing instruments, Graham Eley, who has just joined the scheme as a host, summed up the benefits he has found. 'I have gathered some very simple and practical business initiatives that will help improve our employee communication. Sharing best practice is an excellent source for business improvement. The Simon Jersey visit confirmed my belief that mobilising our employees is key to achieving outstanding business performance.'

Reproduced by permission of Anne Baldwin, Simon Jersey Ltd.

Case Study: Carousel Nurseries

Carousel Nurseries opened in April 1995 at the Leven Valley Enterprise Centre, Dumbarton. There were three children on roll when the business started. A second nursery opened in March 1997. The nurseries serve an area which is not particularly prosperous but which, nonetheless, needs childcare provision to enable parents to go out to work. Until the business was established, childcare in a nursery environment was virtually unobtainable in the area. The company has grown and now has 18 employees and over 120 children on roll.

Carousel Nurseries was set up as a limited company and is currently run by two partners, Anne Jenkins and Claire Rowan. They have spent many years in the retail sector in the roles of

CONTINUED . . . Case Study: Carousel Nurseries

personnel manager and training and development manager respectively.

The mix of expertise in business and child development has proved to be a successful combination for Carousel Nurseries Limited in terms of both quality and financial profitability. The directors believe this will provide a sound platform to achieve the company's aspirations for multi-siting.

'We are unique because we have a different vision of what childcare is, which is different from the "norm". Quality is an integral part of what we do,' said Anne Jenkins.

Carousel needed to enable the business to grow by taking the weight of day-to-day supervision from the partners' shoulders. The Milestone Model of 'Building a Better Business' highlighted the areas where significant changes could be made. A SWOT analysis (Strengths; Weaknesses; Opportunities; Threats) was carried out in the nursery. Among the strengths highlighted were the standard of childcare, quality of staff, artistic flair and innovative creators. The business had good communication skills with a high quality educational programme backed by a good range of resources in terms of equipment and materials. Carousel quickly established a strong reputation and developed a strong link with the local authority.

The analysis pointed to some weaknesses. The location and external appearance of the business itself was not ideal and the lack of available storage space for large items of equipment was a constraint. The directors were feeling very stretched by working long hours and they felt unable to let go and manage. Forward planning to develop systems and staff wasn't mature enough to let the directors ease up and delegate responsibilities. Advertising and marketing to support occupancy during the rapid growth of the business could have been better.

Opportunities were identified in what was an untapped market which could accommodate expansion through the

CONTINUED ... Case Study: Carousel Nurseries

numbers of places to be made available and the range of services offered. The reputation of the business could be used to build its profile further and increase networking opportunities.

Potential threats to the business involved the proximity of competitors in what is a highly competitive sector in most parts of the country. The reputation of the business might be damaged by adverse comments from any dissatisfied customers circulating on the parents' 'grapevine'. Similarly illness of and accidents to children might pose threats if they are misunderstood or misinterpreted.

When the plan for the business was pulled together, the results of this SWOT analysis were taken into account to enable the company to build on its strengths and to address its weaknesses. The Directors attended a 'Better People Better Business' seminar in June 1996 which was hosted by their Local Enterprise Company. The seminar introduced the principles and benefits of Investors in People to them.

They reviewed the requirements of the Standard with their Local Enterprise Company adviser and discussed the possibility of going forward for assessment using their Business Plan as the main evidence instead of the more traditional method of producing a narrative storyboard and portfolio of evidence. Once it was agreed that this was the right way forward for them, they worked their way through the eight elements of 'Building a Better Business' one element at a time. This started with the Business Direction element and ended with all the elements being pulled together in the plan for the business.

During this process an adviser worked closely with them to facilitate and bring to life 'what each element meant for Carousel Nurseries'. It would then be implemented. In this way the time involved with the adviser was kept to an absolute minimum. Once Carousel had successfully implemented each element, they were then ready for the Investors in People assessment. This process was relatively easy as all that was required to be completed was to collate 'live' examples of processes that were in force such as staff appraisal and training planning.

Working through the elements unlocked internal communications in the business. Staff were kept informed through informal staff updates and a full day session was carried out to discuss and agree the content of the plan for the business. Staff became more committed and identified more strongly with the company and what it seeks to achieve. The partners felt that they were becoming more honest with the staff. The culture now is such that there are no 'no-go' areas within the management of the company.

During the implementation of 'Building a Better Business' Anne Jenkins and Claire Rowan initially found it difficult to commit time to the work. But they were surprised to find when they were working with the toolkit, the nurseries were able to run productively in their absence and key results were achieved. Once the toolkit started to be used, the ease with which momentum increased was noticed. Once staff were behind the work, they took off in the same direction and achieved all they set out to. Staff became more responsible for their own training and development and the emphasis in the business now is about staff thinking about their own performance and taking ownership of their development.

The adviser found 'Building a Better Business' easy to implement and easy for staff to understand as it is business focused. The process did not involve a lot of paperwork and was viewed as 'just good practice'. Carousel Nurseries were recognised as an Investor in People on 6 May 1997.

Carousel Nurseries feel that they now have the people and systems to take them to the next stages of growth in their business.

> ### CONTINUED ... Case Study: Carousel Nurseries
>
> 'Everyone is aware of what we are all aspiring to and that the goal-posts are ever moving! We now have the foundation to grow and develop with the systems and good practice we have in place, and these change on a continual basis, as does our business!' said Claire Rowan.
>
> Reproduced by permission of Investors in People UK.

 PAUSE FOR THOUGHT

A flock of birds is a self-contained community, one that follows a set of patterns. There are leaders and there are followers – and sometimes the leaders must drop back into the lead to carry the burden of the winds.

Because of the intuitive nature of the birds, they know when to be the leader and when to be a part of the team. From amid the chaos of hundreds of birds taking off and landing together emerges an orderly system of organising, motivating, and communication without word.

Managers can emulate this 'order from chaos' method, because communicating and motivating come in different forms than the conventional way of thinking. (Daft, 1999)

Leadership in the Twenty-first Century

In small businesses some entrepreneurs exercise power to manage their businesses. They believe that because they own the business or because they have appointed managers they have leaders in their organisations. Power-driven leadership is self-focused. The alternative form of leadership is responsibility driven.

An effective leader has to generate trust and have a sense of purpose. They have to face the challenges of globalisation and new technology.

> **KEY CONCEPT**
>
> Effective leaders face the challenges of globalisation and new technology.

Leadership has to be looked at as a holistic concept. There has to be a focus on attributes such as values, credibility, power, integrity, ability to see the whole picture and ability to motivate staff.

If the leader and employees share the same values and they internalise these values, the bond between leader and employees will be strong. In a situation like this staff will freely communicate in order to transfer their knowledge.

Leadership in a knowledge-driven organisation has to be a matter of substance, not style.

A leader in any type of organisation should:

> **KEY CONCEPT**
>
> Leadership in a knowledge-driven organisation has to be a matter of substance, not style.

- Act as a coach.
- Free up information and encourage knowledge creation.
- Provide resources to show commitment.
- Take part in the learning organisation.
- Get rid of a blame culture.
- Reward and recognise the efforts of his/her staff.
- Facilitate individual and team development.
- Share the vision and involve people in strategy formulation.
- Listen for various possibilities.

Peter Senge, a guru on the learning organisation, writes:

Imagine that your organisation is an ocean liner and that you are 'the leader'. What is your role?

I have asked this question of groups of managers many times. The most common answer, not surprisingly, is 'the captain'. Others say, 'the navigator', setting the direction. Still others say 'the helmsman', actually controlling the direction, or 'the engineer' down there stoking the fire, providing energy, or 'the social director' making sure everybody's enrolled, involved and communicating. While these are legitimate leadership roles, there is another which, in many ways, eclipses them all in importance. Yet rarely does any one mention it.

The neglected leadership role is the designer of the ship. No one has more sweeping influence than the designer. What good does it do for the captain to say, 'turn starboard 30 degrees' when the designer has built a rudder that will only turn to port, or which takes six hours to turn to starboard? It's fruitless to be the leader in an organisation that is poorly designed. (Senge, 1998)

A 'due diligence' audit on leadership for business should look like that in Table 6.1.

Table 6.1 *Leadership balance sheet*

Assets	Liabilities
Honesty	Greed
Integrity	Macho
Communication	Ruthlessness
Competence	Numbers orientation
Trustworthiness	Arrogance
Consideration	Insularity
Support	Fear
Caring	Intimidation
Passion for customers	lack of inspiration
Recognition	Manipulation
Visibility	Control freak
Respect	Scandal

For best practice leadership ask your employees to assess you.

Measuring the effectiveness of your leadership

Award 1 point for 'yes' and 2 points for 'no'.

1 Is he/she an insular leader, keeping to himself/herself?
2 Does he/she speak to you regularly?
3 Is he/she competent in what he/she does?
4 Do you know what his/her values are?
5 Has he/she communicated his/her values clearly to all employees in the organisation?
6 Can you trust him/her?
7 Does he/she trust you?

8   Is he/she fair in dealing with customers?

9   Is he/she fair in dealing with his/her employees?

10 Is he/she supportive in a crisis?

11 Does he/she consider himself/herself as a 'servant' to others?

12 Do people inside and outside the organisation respect him/her?

13 Does he/she understand the nature of the changing market and business environment?

14 Does he/she recognise the efforts of all employees?

15 Does he/she project a macho image?

16 Is he/she ruthless in making decisions?

17 Does he/she treat you with dignity?

18 Is he/she a good communicator?

19 Does he/she stimulate employees to gain new competencies and skills?

20 Does he/she lead by example?

21 Does he/she blame his/her employees when things go wrong?

22 Does he/she promote collaboration within the organisation?

23 Does he/she take a direct interest in the type of people recruited?

24 Does he/she encourage knowledge sharing?

25 Does he/she believe in open and honest communication?

Scoring.

25–23 points. You have a very effective leader. Congratulations.

22–20 points. You have a very good leader. Some room for improvement.

19–15 points. You have an average leader. Must focus attention on being effective.

Below 15 points. You have a long way to go before the leader becomes effective.

Leadership and Culture

Designing an organisation involves having a vision and core values. These are the key attributes that underpin corporate culture and the learning organisation.

Corporate culture provides the context within which business decisions are made and implemented. It can be expressed as 'the way we do business around here'. It is very important for a knowledge-driven organisation to be flexible in order to respond to market needs. Organisational culture can facilitate such flexibility or it can be a big hindrance.

> **KEY CONCEPT**
>
> Designing an organisation involves having a vision and core values.

Organisational culture can be categorised into collaborative culture; cooperative culture; co-existence culture; and conflict culture.

> **KEY CONCEPT**
>
> It is very important for a knowledge-driven organisation to be flexible in order to respond to market needs.

- *Collaborative culture*: In this type of culture people enjoy sharing information and helping one another.
- *Cooperative culture*. Employees cooperate when necessary but the degree of interpersonal communication is low.
- *Co-existence culture*. Employees tolerate one another because they have to but the flow of information is very restricted.
- *Conflict culture*. There is constant backbiting and numerous hidden agendas.

The culture of a knowledge-driven organisation has to be collaborative in order to promote free flows of information and facilitate knowledge creation.

An effective leader has to focus attention on organisational culture, in relation to the shared beliefs, values and expectations of the people in the organisation. It influences the performance of every individual and consequently affects organisational performance.

An appropriate culture:

- Creates a sense of identity.
- Enhances commitment to the organisation's mission.
- Reinforces standards of behaviour.

What is an appropriate culture?

The culture of a knowledge-driven organisation has to involve:

- Tolerance.
- Empowerment.
- Trust.
- Networking.
- open communication.
- Recognition.
- Diversity.
- Talented individuals.

Culture is an intangible asset of an organisation. It provides and enhances organisational capability. Without a collaborative and flexible culture, organisations will not be best placed to respond to environmental changes.

A flexible culture does not mean flexible and changing values, however. Values underpin culture; what does change is the means of responding to market needs. This could result in altering the structure of an organisation or 'the way we work around here'. In other words, leadership has to attack a 'not invented here' attitude.

> **KEY CONCEPT**
>
> Culture is an intangible asset of an organisation. It provides and enhances organisational capability.

Empowerment

Empowerment became a buzzword in the 1980s. In practice there is often a confusion between empowerment and delegation.

The *Oxford English Dictionary* defines delegation as 'entrusting authority to a deputy'. In management terms delegation implies breaking down responsibility into tasks; analysing tasks to measure whether they are

> **KEY CONCEPT**
>
> In practice there is often a confusion between empowerment and delegation.

suitable for being carried out by specific individuals; and assessing individuals to see whether they are suited to assume the authority.

Guidelines for effective delegation

- Consider the 'responsibility' to be delegated.
- Analyse the responsibility in terms of separate tasks and write them down.
- Write down which of these tasks can be delegated and which have to be done by yourself.
- List those that have to be done by you and decide their order of importance and urgency.
- Set a time scale for yourself for completion of your tasks.
- List the individuals to whom you could delegate tasks.
- Be very clear in your objectives and desired outcomes.
- Set a time scale for individuals to whom you are delegating.
- If the person to whom you want to delegate is willing to do the job but is not confident or lacks ability, decide whether he or she could be coached or trained within the time scale.

Barriers to delegation

- I like doing it myself.
- I can do it better than anyone else.
- I cannot explain what I want.
- I do not have time to coach or guide.
- Insecurity.
- I can't tolerate mistakes.
- Envy of subordinate ability.
- Lack of organisational skill.
- Failure to follow up: people do what we inspect not what we expect.

Empowerment, in contrast to delegation, is about releasing human energy and trusting an individual to make decisions. In a knowledge-driven organisation it is important to empower your staff in order to give them the power to make quick decisions and to gain their commitment and involvement.

> **KEY CONCEPT**
>
> Empowerment is about releasing human energy and trusting an individual to make decisions.

Empowerment is based on the assumptions that:

- Employees want responsibility.
- They want to own a problem.
- They understand the corporate mission.
- They feel that they are trusted.

Empowerment is about creating situations where workers share power and assume the responsibility of making decisions for the benefit of customers and their organisations.

> **KEY CONCEPT**
>
> In empowerment *trust* plays a key role.

In empowerment *trust* plays a key role.

 ## BENCHMARKING: the key success factors for empowerment

- There must be information sharing, including of sensitive information.
- There should be appropriate leadership that can facilitate empowerment.
- There is a need for team-building.
- Employees should be trained to behave as entrepreneurs.
- Employees should understand the challenges facing their businesses.
- Top management should trust their employees.
- Employees in turn should give their full commitment.
- The organisational culture should allow employees to make mistakes and learn from their mistakes.
- Leaders should be honest and give effective performance feedback.
- It is important to establish the parameters for decision making.

- The organisation should make 'finger-pointing' obsolete. If you find a problem you own it.

Do not empower for the sake of empowerment. Don't jump on to the bandwagon of another management fad. Only introduce the opportunity of empowerment if the business requires it and as long as you train your staff and support the process by coaching and providing effective leadership.

Good communication is also important to persuade employees to buy into what the organisation is trying to do. At Toyota, for example, at least two sessions are set aside for daily communication. Group leaders start the day by explaining the work schedule and giving any company news. Quite often the group leader uses this opportunity to involve the team in solving a problem. Toyota believes that managers have to be trained to become facilitators.

 ## PAUSE FOR THOUGHT

This is a story about four people named Everybody, Somebody, Anybody and Nobody.

There was an important job to be done to improve customer service and Everybody was sure that Somebody would do it.

Anybody could have done it, but Nobody did it. Somebody got angry about that, because it was Everybody's job. Everybody thought Anybody could do it.

But Nobody realised that Everybody wouldn't do it.

It ended up that Everybody blamed Somebody when Nobody did what Anybody could have done. *(Source Unknown)*.

Empowerment has to have SMART dimensions:

S It has to be supported by top management.

M Employees have to be motivated.

A Authority has to be aligned to strategic direction.

R Responsibility is important in empowerment.

T Trust your staff.

Empowerment is part of organisational culture and an intangible asset of the organisation. In the next chapter we examine other key intangible assets.

SEVEN

Knowledge, Intangible Assets and Superior Performance

At the end of each day a company's most expensive assets walk out though the door.

Overview

- Superior business performance depends on tangible as well as intangible assets.
- Intangible assets consist of people, customers, culture, brands, processes and proprietary technology.
- Organisations have to take steps to build knowledge of their intangible assets that they can leverage to compete effectively.
- Care should be taken when recruiting people and after recruiting a strategy should be in place to retain them.
- Attention should be paid to managing the psychological contract that comes into existence when individuals join organisations.
- Consider what makes people tick and take appropriate steps to motivate staff.
- Customers are the reason for a business's existence. Take steps to build knowledge of customers.
- Do not neglect brands if you have them. Brands add value to your business if they are properly managed.
- Finally, processes, technology and innovation should be used to enhance business performance.

An organisation's assets can be categorised as tangible and intangible. Tangible assets, such as buildings, plant, factories, machinery and stocks, feature in a balance sheet, which show what a company owes (liabilities) and what it owns (assets).

The focus of attention in valuing any company is generally on its financial performance. The balance sheet is a financial snapshot of a business at a particular time and the profit and loss account shows how the company has traded in the year it is reporting (see Chapter 8).

The general performance indicators of a company are return on capital employed (which measures earning power and shows how the company has used the total funds available to it), profit margin (sales revenue minus cost of sales), stock turnover (how quickly stock is converted into sales), the current ratio (what resources are available to meet its liabilities) and so on.

The demand for keeping financial records has existed since trade began. Financial performance reflects how an organisation is controlling and monitoring its organisational objectives and its operations. Some argue that the whole rationale of a commercial organisation is to make profit. The organisation, therefore, owes it to its stakeholders, including its employees, to remain solvent and to achieve what it has set out in its plan.

There is no argument against this. However, the complexity of business is increasing and its very nature is changing. For example, training shoe manufacturer Nike believes that its main business is to convert ideas into physical goods. Best practice is thus also to focus on intangible assets.

> **KEY CONCEPT**
>
> Intangible assets play a great role in enhancing business capability.

Intangible assets play a great role in enhancing business capability. But what are they?

The intangible assets of every business consists of its:

- People and knowledge.
- Customers.
- Culture.

- Brands.
- Processes.
- Proprietary technology and innovation.

People are our greatest asset: hype or reality?

Many organisations pay lip service to such sentiment. Knowledge in any organisation rests with people. Without people there will be no ideas and no innovation. It is their tacit knowledge, when transformed and embedded in processes and systems, that creates organisational knowledge.

> **KEY CONCEPT**
>
> Knowledge in any organisation rests with its people. Without people there will be no ideas and no innovation.

In an organisation that is operating in the new economy, talent becomes a very scarce resource. If you want your workers to make decisions close to the customer and take responsibility, then you have to manage them differently.

> **KEY CONCEPT**
>
> It is important to pay attention to the type of workers you are recruiting.

But before then it is important to pay attention to the type of workers you are recruiting. If you want your organisation to be knowledge driven, look for people who:

- Are talented.
- Love challenges and are willing to experiment.
- Have aspirations and values.
- Are willing to share their experience and tacit knowledge.
- Respect their colleagues;
- Are able to establish relationships with their partners and customers.
- willing to upgrade their skills and acquire new skills
- Are flexible.

These are the attributes that need to be paid attention to at the time of recruitment. Also, if you are recruiting any senior person, then top management must be involved in the selection.

Once you have recruited your staff you should have a policy in place to retain them. When people leave they walk away with knowledge. Remember that it is not possible to transform all tacit knowledge, however willing an employee is, into explicit knowledge. Therefore it is always good policy to hold on to your staff as long as possible.

> **KEY CONCEPT**
>
> When people leave they walk away with knowledge.

Benefits of retaining staff

- Recruitment is a very costly process.
- You want to sustain your training and development investment and gain from its returns.
- Staff turnover affects team spirit.
- Customer relationships are damaged if there is too much staff turnover.
- Staff attrition has a domino effect inside the organisation.
- Staff turnover reduces the rate of product development and innovation.

Retaining your staff is about continuous motivation. How do you motivate your staff continuously? People join an organisation because they want to fulfil their needs and aspirations. A psychological contract comes into existence as soon as they join any organisation.

> **KEY CONCEPT**
>
> Retaining your staff is about continuous motivation.

The psychological contract

Individuals expect:

- A salary.
- Personal development.

> **KEY CONCEPT**
>
> Psychological contract comes into existence as soon as an employee joins any organisation.

- Challenges.
- Recognition.
- Security.
- Fairness.
- A conducive working environment.
- Respect.

Organisations, on the other hand, expect:

- An honest day's work.
- Loyalty.
- Initiative.
- Conformity.
- Job effectiveness.
- Flexibility.
- Willingness to learn.

Managing and matching two sets of expectations is what leadership is all about. Effective leadership, therefore, plays a significant role in motivation and staff retention.

There are many theories of motivation, but most of them have limitations when applied in practice. If you are an effective leader along the lines indicated in Chapter 6 and you are aware of your employees' expectations, then managing them is what motivation is all about in practice.

> **KEY CONCEPT**
>
> Managing and matching two sets of expectations is what leadership is all about.

 ## PAUSE FOR THOUGHT: What makes people tick?

People issues are becoming critical in managing every type and size of business. Many strategic alliances and mergers fail because of clashes of corporate culture, mistrust or lack of synergy, for example.

Organisations are creating alliances or opting for mergers in order to extend market share, gain access to new markets or acquire new technologies or capabilities etc. They also delayer and empower people in order to be responsive to market needs. Such measures create insecurity and lack of trust among employees.

Successful organisational transformation depends on the capabilities and competencies of staff.

Gaining the support and trust of your people

Undertake a staff audit

The SWOT technique can be used creatively to undertake a staff audit. The following issues can surface when using this technique.

- *Strengths*. Staff loyalty, enthusiasm, willing to take more responsibility, skills, willing to learn and develop etc.
- *Weaknesses*. Ambiguity of role due to various changes, stress, overload of work, 'nine-to-five' attitude in some cases, excessive overtime etc.
- *Opportunities*. Succession, training and development etc.
- *Threats*. Staff headhunted, lack of motivation, burn-out syndrome etc.

These represent your perception of your staff. It will be a very useful exercise to undertake a staff audit with your staff. If you have a large number of staff then the exercise can be conducted with your senior staff and direct reports.

The advantage of doing this will be to show if there is any discrepancy between your perception and that of your staff. Involving your staff will also act as motivation.

Understand their strengths and weaknesses

Having identified the strengths and weaknesses, the next step is to take them on board when formulating a performance system.

Remember that performance is influenced by the interrelationship between resources and capabilities. Organisations need to be able to use their resources effectively in order to build and enhance their capabilities. Resources and capabilities underpin strategy.

As we saw in Chapter 4, performance appraisal should indicate *what is expected* (outcomes) of an individual, *why it is expected*, by *when it is expected, how outcomes are going to be measured* and by whom.

Performance is a function of:

- *Knowing what to do* (job clarification).
- *Knowing how to do it* (job skills). Strengths should be capitalised on and weaknesses should be minimised in terms of developing staff
- *Wanting to do it* (motivation). If your staff feel you do care about them and involve them in the staff audit, they will be motivated to do the job.
- *Having an opportunity to do it* (support). All staff need support from their bosses. Without an opportunity to show how they can use their skills, staff will be frustrated.

Many experts agree that more attention needs to be paid to 'people issues'. This is not that difficult. What is important is getting your staff to contribute to corporate objectives. Once you undersrand their strengths and weaknesses you need to demonstrate that you want to develop their capabilities and treat them fairly.

Involve your staff in preparing performance objectives
Ask your staff to come up with key objectives relating to the tasks they perform.

Build staff's aspirations, training, capabilities and development into your measurement system
Use performance appraisal as a developmental tool (see Chapter 4).

Provide development opportunities
Those who are able and willing should be given an opportunity to develop in order to enhance their competencies. It is important to provide relevant training and coaching opportunities for your staff.

Introduce impact analysis

Introduce impact analysis to your staff and get them involved in capturing external changes (see Chapter 2) and understanding their impact on what they are doing. This will introduce a culture of change and they will be actively involved.

Introducing any change internally requires a significant amount of preparation. Consultancy McKinsey, for example, uses the 7S method to chart the impact of change internally and addresses all 7Ss in order to introduce change successfully.

The 7Ss are strategy, structure, systems, staff, style, shared values and skills.

- *Strategy*: analysis of environment, competition and strengths and weaknesses.
- *Structure*: salient features of the organisational chart, patterns of functions, status, communication and control.
- *Systems*: the operational systems in place in the organisation.
- *Staff*: competencies and different functions (engineers, account-ants, managers etc.).
- *Style*: management style.
- *Shared values*: Corporate culture and shared values in relation to quality, customers, employees etc.
- *Skills*: distinctive capabilities of the organisation that authentically differentiate it from competition.

If you are going to bring about any changes in your organisation, these need to be assessed in relation to their impact on the 7Ss.

The other technique that can be used is *force field analysis*. This involves mapping driving forces (things that are going to drive the desired change) and restraining forces (the roadblocks to change).

To implement change, management needs to analyse the forces that will drive that change. By selecting and removing the forces that restrain change, the driving forces will be strong enough to enable implementation. As restraining forces are reduced or removed, behaviour will change to incorporate the desired changes.

For example, a company that wanted to change from a traditional to a just-in-time inventory system found that the driving forces associated with implementation were cost savings from reduced inventories, savings from needing fewer workers, better customer response etc., while the restraining forces were resistance from the union, the existing freight system that was too slow to deliver inventory on time, workers were not skilled enough to handle a just-in-time system etc.

Force field analysis involves identifying information relating to the following steps:

1 The situation as it is now.
2 The situation as I want it to be.
3 What will keep the situation from changing?
4 What are the roadblocks?
5 What resources will I need to achieve my objectives?

There is always some resistance to change. Research has shown that the best methods of overcoming resistance are as follows:

- *Communication and education*. Explain why change is necessary and what you are going to do in order to provide support.
- *Participation and involvement*. Those involved should be motivated to become driving forces.
- *Negotiation*. There ought be some give and take. Negotiate and satisfy the question of 'What's in it for me?'.

Those employees who have a high degree of trust but are highly dissatisfied with the status quo will provide no resistance. They could become 'change champions'.

In contrast, those who distrust the company and are very satisfied with the status quo will pose a great challenge to you because they are the resistors.

Those who have a low degree of trust in the organisation but at the same time are not happy with the status quo will be 'foot draggers'. In this case you have to win their trust by education and communication.

Change affects the terms of the psychological contract with employees. To win support and create a driving force, the changes in the terms of psychological contract have to be perceived to be favourable to employees.

Motivate staff

Staff are motivated when they know that the organisation they work for does care for them and has introduced the change after careful analysis and when, where appropriate, they have been consulted and/or involved.

Customers

Without customers there is no business. As we saw in Chapter 4, organisations should make every attempt to create knowledge about their customers:

- Who are your customers?
- What do they buy from you?
- How much do they spend with you?
- What are their needs and expectations?
- Do you meet them?
- What do you need to do to win and sustain their loyalty?

Best practice in this case will be to benchmark against the 'best in class' organisation or within your own organisation, or to benchmark against the model that you and your staff have created.

> **KEY CONCEPT**
>
> Adopting best practice will lead to the creation of customer knowledge – one of your organisation's most valuable intangible assets.

Adopting best practice will lead to the creation of customer knowledge – one of your organisation's most valuable intangible assets.

 PAUSE FOR THOUGHT

A few years ago, when things were not going well for carrier company DHL, it decided to do away with the functional allocation of responsibilities and created mini-businesses at the lowest possible level in order to take decision making closer to customers. In the process the company eliminated several layers of management, moving from a structure where the managing director was seven levels away from the courier to one where he is four levels away.

Understanding customers, listen and learn are the watchwords at DHL. The company invests in research to gain in-depth understanding of their customers' needs.

DHL also instituted a 'cradle to grave' policy in relation to building customer knowledge. This is an approach to communication planning that is responsive to the current requirements and potential of a customer as their relationship with a supplier grows. The policy is designed to establish where in the customer life cycle DHL is currently sitting to tailor its communications precisely to address that position.

When Louis V. Gerstner took over as head of IBM, he said to *Business Week* (9th December, 1996), 'I came here with a view that you start the day with customers, that you start thinking about the company around its customers, and you organise around customers.'

Culture

As we saw in Chapter 6, managing knowledge is about creating an environment within your organisation so that people can openly share their experience and transfer knowledge.

The culture has to be appropriate for knowledge to be created and transferred. This is one of the key responsibilities of an effective leader and this is what culture is all about.

'The way we do business around here' has to be flexible enough to respond to external changes and meet market needs. Culture is one of the sources of organisational capability and it is, therefore, an intangible asset.

> **KEY CONCEPT**
>
> Culture is one of the sources of organisational capability and it is, therefore, an intangible asset.

'The way we do business around here' incorporates:

- The way you treat your employees.
- The way you treat your customers.
- The way you treat your business partners.
- The way your board is constituted.
- The way people are promoted.
- The way people are selected.
- The way new staff are inducted.
- The way efforts are made to retain your staff.
- The way staff performance is measured.
- The way customers' needs are measured.
- The way employees treat one another.
- The way employees are rewarded.
- The way employees are motivated and empowered.
- The way decisions and policies are communicated.

The list could go on. Because culture has numerous dimensions and incorporates behavioural aspects, many businesses find it very difficult to think of culture as an asset.

Case Study: A culture of sharing at Costain

Costain, one of the UK's leading international engineering and construction organisations, has visited many Inside UK Enterprise (IUKE) – Construction host companies. The company's Business Improvement Manager, Terry Sexton, said:

'Costain's enthusiasm for such visits is testament to our continuous improvement philosophy – it's not limited to one project or one particular period of time. Continuous improvement requires continous learning. I have found the visits invaluable and as a result, at a corporate level we are implementing a number of improvement techniques.'

> ## CONTINUED ... Case Study: A culture of sharing at Costain
>
> Costain has visited a variety of host companies including Stent, John Laing and Amey. Future visits planned include Morrison Construction, WS Atkins and Gardiner & Theobald. Host companies also benefit from being involved. For example, Tony Merricks, Chairman of Stent said: 'These visits are a first class idea. Not only have we benefited as a host company from the feedback from our visitors, we have also used the programme of visits to other companies to keep our management team on the pulse of the latest developments in the industry. What better way to learn than directly from the innovators themselves?'
>
> 'But the most appealing aspect was the culture of sharing and the open forum for discussion that was fostered. No-one was point scoring or worried about losing their competitive advantage. Everyone wanted the best for the industry. It was reassuring to see that we are working towards the same issues. We all understood that by collaborating, everybody can benefit,' said Mr Sexton.
>
> Mr Sexton is using the ideas gleaned from the visits as part of Costain's constant drive to use best practice methods. 'It's been challenging at times – culture changes always are. It's too early to talk about cost and time savings, but the IUKE visits are certainly in tune with our best practice philosophy.'
>
> Taken from the CBI's *Fit for the Future* web site during 2001: www.fitforthefuture.co.uk
> Reproduced by permission of the CBI. [Costain are no longer participating in the IUKE.]

Brands

Not many small and medium-sized enterprises have brands, but those that do should consider them as intangible assets.

A brand is a name, sign, symbol or design or a combination of these intended

> **KEY CONCEPT**
>
> A brand communicates attributes, benefits, personality and values.

to reflect and communicate the values of products, services or the organisation. A brand communicates attributes (such as speed, quality, durability) benefits (such as comfort, safety), personality (matching the desired self-image of buyers with the brand's image) and values.

Companies such as Coca-Cola, McDonald's, Sony, Kodak, Walt Disney, Virgin, Body Shop and McKinsey have become world leaders through the strength of their brands. Similarly, products such as Nescafé, Levi's and Kellogg's have become bestsellers due to their brands.

Brands don't only represent organisations, products and services. When celebrities are used to promote certain products or services, 'personal brands' come into existence.

Consumers establish a set of beliefs about a particular brand. These beliefs are based on perceptions, which in turn create expectations. What organisations have to do is manage these expectations.

To use a brand as an intangible asset, a business has to build knowledge on how its brand is perceived by its customers and what the brand means to those customers. Surveys should be conducted to gather this information.

> **KEY CONCEPT**
>
> To use a brand as an intangible asset, a business has to build knowledge on how its brand is perceived by its customers.

If brand image is managed well it can enhance the value of a business. Some companies, such as General Electric, Intel and Microsoft, have significantly higher market values than their 'book' or accounting values because of the strength of their brands.

 BENCHMARKING: Managing a brand effectively

- Communicate the nature of the brand within your organisation.
- Let your staff buy into what the brand stands for.
- Communicate the value of your brand to your partners, including your distributors.
- Deliver what is perceived by consumers – what customers perceive, customers should receive.

- Undertake regular surveys to gain information on your brands from your customers' perspective.
- Put processes in place to deliver brand equity.

Processes

Processes incorporate knowledge. The 'value chain' of an organisation reflects how values are added at each stage of production. It involves various processes and associated activities.

> **KEY CONCEPT**
>
> Processes incorporate knowledge.

Best practice is to examine all activities within each process and eliminate those activities that do not add value. In this way your processes become key intangible assets.

Kodak, for example, reengineered its product development process by introducing concurrent engineering. Subsequently it introduced a new disposable camera in 35 rather than 70 weeks.

Processes also constitute organisational capability and enable organisations to gain and sustain superior performance.

Case study: Sainsbury's supply chain – an invisible asset

Sainsbury's supermarkets, with the help of Microsoft Certified Solution Provider EQOS Systems, has recently launched a new supply chain initiative for all its suppliers to boost efficiency and communication. The Internet-based information sharing and collaboration system, which has recently gone live, will eventually allow all 4,000 Sainsbury's suppliers to strive towards the Efficient Consumer Response (ECR) principle of integrated supply and demand. The solution, the first retail system of its kind in the UK to be based on the Microsoft Value Chain Initiative, also has the scope to be dramatically extended in the future, to allow for efficient new product introduction to the

CONTINUED ... Case study: Sainsbury's supply chain – an invisible asset

shop floor, better product promotion planning and co-managed forecasting across the supply chain.

Customer perceptions of a retail organisation can drive the success or failure of retail outlets. Whether it be the quality or freshness of produce sold in the store, or lack of vegetarian or organic goods, supply is driven by the desires of the consumer. Recent initiatives, such as Sainsbury's 'Orderline' home shopping, Sainsbury's Bank and the Reward Points scheme, are all proving successful in improving customer loyalty and increasing the offerings Sainsbury's can bring to the market place. Inevitably, however, a company will only survive if it offers the best service and quality in its core business. Recently, Sainsbury's has implemented a solution with the help of EQOS Systems Limited, which is a member of the Value Chain Initiative (VCI), a supply chain-based industry initiative sponsored by Microsoft. Members of the VCI are retailers and Microsoft solutions providers who develop line of business applications within the supply chain using Microsoft technologies.

The visible service Sainsbury's provides to customers can only be as good as the invisible supply chain that supports it. To this end, Sainsbury's invests a significant amount of time and money in assessing best practice in all of its operations, including Logistics Management. John Rowe, Director of Logistics at Sainsbury's, set up Logistics three years ago, with the specific task of centralising the management of logistics and assessing how the supply chain could be more effectively managed.

He explains: 'When I joined Sainsbury's, supply chain logistics was managed in three separate functions; distribution, trading and retail. My remit was to re-engineer this into one single group and one single process, in order to optimise the supply chain.' Sainsbury's is aiming for Just in Time (JIT) supply, which means a continuous flow of products as and when outlets need them.

CONTINUED ... Case study: Sainsbury's supply chain – an invisible asset

There are over 400 people supporting Logistics, with half the group focused on business processes and the other half focused on IT systems development. The group structures itself into joint teams to drive projects with a clear business focus.

Since John Rowe's appointment, there has been a gradual change in the way Sainsbury's has worked with its suppliers and partners. A significant focus of Sainsbury's drive to satisfy the consumer is based on what is known as Efficient Consumer Response (ECR). Originally an initiative driven from the United States and adopted in Europe in 1994 (see http://www.ecr-europe.com/), ECR aims to provide the retail consumer with best quality service through integrated partner collaboration, information sharing and efficient supply-chain operations. Hence, this drive towards ECR cannot be fulfilled by Sainsbury's alone, as it relies on the retailer's and supplier's supply chain providing products in a JIT way. Therefore, the accurate and timely sharing of information between the systems of different parties within the chain is essential to ECR.

ECR has been a philosophy in practice within the retail market in the UK for about two years and Sainsbury's has embraced it, as have other major retailers. John Rowe explains: 'The use of ECR principles is extremely beneficial in a number of areas, but particularly important to us is the benefits it brings to product promotions. ECR has estimated that across Europe $4 billion can be saved from efficient promotions. With so many people involved in a process inefficiencies are inevitable. The benefits from resolving these can therefore be immense.'

Estimating customer response to a new line or product promotion is difficult and sometimes expensive. ECR encourages retailers and suppliers to share information in real time on the performance of promotions from day one, thus enabling the most correct estimation of stock levels, as well as dictating

> ## CONTINUED ... Case study: Sainsbury's supply chain – an invisible asset
>
> correct production levels to the supplier. Therefore, it can also significantly reduce product waste, especially within the perishable goods market or high residual stock in non perishable.
>
> John Rowe continues: 'ECR also opened up communications between Sainsbury's and its suppliers. It was no longer just a conversation about best price. There is much more sharing of information and joint decision making. It was logical therefore that we should develop systems to communicate essential information with our major suppliers and, eventually, with the rest of the chain.'
>
> With the new EQOS system, Sainsbury's will be able to place new lines of goods, as well as product promotions, in stores in a much shorter time. Quantities can be predicted and managed in a much more accurate way, whereas previously there was a difficulty in matching the correct stock to demand ratios. John Rowe adds: 'Now we can co-manage forecasts with our suppliers, whereas previously we worked in isolation. Branded suppliers will have far more of an idea about what the impact of the advertising plans are, promotions they are running, and so on, so we can let them update our forecasts of their products on a continuous basis.'
>
> Reproduced by permission of *Management Today*, Haymarket Business Publishing.

Proprietary technology and innovation

Proprietary technology, consisting of patents, copyrights and trade secrets, constitutes an intangible asset. Knowledge is embedded in technology.

Some forms of knowledge, once embedded in products, processes and symbols, can be legally protected to stop its abuse by competitors. When knowledge is embedded in products, processes and documents, it is

> **KEY CONCEPT**
>
> Proprietary technology, consisting of patents, copyrights and trade secrets, constitutes an intangible asset.

transformed into intellectual property. Inventions, trade marks, and industrial designs constitute industrial property and they are protected by registration.

Copyright, which deals mainly with literary works, photographic and audio-visual works, musical and artistic works does not have to be registered to be legally protected.

The World Intellectual Property Organisation (WIPO), a specialised agency of the United Nations, is the world body responsible for promoting the protection of intellectual property by means of inter-governmental cooperation. In addition, the World Trade Organisation (WTO) administers the Trade-Related Aspects of Intellectual Property Rights (TRIPS) agreement, including trade in counterfeit goods.

 PAUSE FOR THOUGHT

Richard Thoman, who was appointed CEO of the $20 billion Xerox Corporation in the summer of 1999, believes that one of the strategic keys to Xerox's future is something so intangible, so invisible to traditional bottom-line thinking and corporate practice, that it doesn't even show up on the balance sheet.

His focus is on intellectual property. He believes that intellectual property is going to add value not only at Xerox but increasingly at other companies who want to win.

Dow Chemical's efforts to catalogue nearly 30 000 patents brought it $40 million in savings and enabled the company to enter into $1 billion of new licensing agreements. Dow first began exploring new ways to manage intellectual assets five years ago.

Innovation

In 1985 Peter Drucker wrote:

Innovation is the specific tool of entrepreneurs, the means by which they exploit change as an opportunity for a different business or a different service. It is capable of being presented as a discipline, capable of being learned, capable of being practised. Entrepreneurs need to search purposefully for the sources of information, the changes and their symptoms that indicate opportunities to successful innovation. And they need to know and to apply the principles of successful innovation.

When knowledge is created in an organisation it becomes a resource and its use could create new products or new processes.

Knowledge and innovation are a two-way process – knowledge is a source of innovation and innovation in turn becomes the source of new knowledge.

Innovation involves:

- Gathering information.
- Transforming information into knowledge.
- Sharing and transferring this knowledge.
- Embedding the knowledge into products or services and processes.
- Bringing these into being (invention).
- Using this invention in practice (innovation).

Innovators come up with ideas. It is important to record these ideas and share information on who knows what. If these ideas are not recorded the business loses the knowledge – it walks away when the person leaves the organisation.

Innovation is not just about products, services and processes. It also means new ways of looking at things. Some companies have strategies and processes in place to tap into their staff's knowledge as a source of ideas. If staff see that their companies value their contribution they become motivated and the company in turn benefits.

> **KEY CONCEPT**
>
> Innovation is not just about products, services and processes. It also means new ways of looking at things.

It is reported that an employee of match manufacturer Swan Vesta who offered to save 50% of production costs and at the same time give the product a unique selling point was on the right lines. When asked what his idea was, he simply said: 'Put the strike face on one side of the match box only'. Brilliant!

 PAUSE FOR THOUGHT

At conglomerate 3M corporate targets demand that 30% of its annual revenue come from products that are less than four years old.

Compensation for senior and divisional managers is also tied to the percentage of sales from new products.

The company requires all employees to set aside 15% of their work time to pursue personal research interests.

The 11th commandment of 3M is: 'Thou shalt not kill new ideas for products.'

Leaders in the company see themselves as keepers of the values.

EIGHT

Measuring
Intangible Assets

What gets measured gets managed.

Overview

- Organisations generally measure their assets and performance from a financial perspective.
- There is a need to measure intangible assets from various perspectives.
- Various methods are proposed and full guidance are given on measuring intangible assets.
- Among the methods proposed are the Business Excellence Method, the Balanced Scorecard, the Skandia Navigator and the Intangible Assets Monitor.
- Comments are also made in relation to measuring brands.

Organisations generally measure their success and performance in financial terms. The profit and loss account and balance sheet constitute their main financial documents.

A balance sheet gives information on assets and liabilities. Assets are divided into fixed assets and current assets. Fixed assets are those that have been acquired for use in the business, for example plant and machinery, while current assets are cash and other items that will be converted into cash, for example stocks and debtors.

From the balance sheet various ratios can be calculated to assess the liquidity and solvency of the business.

A profit and loss account provides a summary of how the company has traded in the year it is reporting. It deals with items such as turnover and trading profit.

Ideally this financial accounting model should have been expanded to incorporate the valuation of a company's intangible and intellectual assets, such as high-quality products and services, motivated and skilled employees, responsive and predictable internal processes, and satisfied and loyal customers. Such a valuation of intangible assets and company capabilities would be especially helpful since, for information age companies, these assets are more critical to success than traditional physical and tangible assets. If intangible assets of the companies were within the financial accounting model, organisations that enhanced these assets and capabilities could communicate this improvement to employees, shareholders, creditors, and communities. Conversely, when companies depleted their stock of intangible assets and capabilities, the negative effect could be reflected immediately in the income statement. Realistically, however, difficulties in placing a reliable financial value on such assets as the new product pipeline; process capabilities; employees' skills, motivation and flexibility; customer loyalty; data bases; and systems will likely preclude them from ever being recognised in organisational balance sheets. Yet these are the very assets and capabilities that are critical for success in today's and tomorrow's competitive environment. (Kaplan and Norton, 1996)

> **KEY CONCEPT**
>
> For information age companies, these assets are more critical to success than traditional physical and tangible assets.

Organisations should value their intangible assets and it is also important that they measure their effectiveness. Some organisations, for example, already use the Business Excellence Model to enhance their performance and others use the Balanced Scorecard to measure their performance. Both these measurement models can be used to measure intangible assets.

Business Excellence Model

The Business Excellence Model was formerly known as the European Quality Foundation Model of the European Foundation for Quality Management. This Foundation was established in 1988 with the aim of improving the competitiveness of European companies in the world market.

The model was developed in 1990 and now forms the framework for sustained competitive advantage. In the UK the British Quality Foundation was established in 1992 and it is the custodian of the Business Excellence Model.

The model consists of five 'enablers' and four 'results' areas. The superior performance of any business depends on its general business performance, customer satisfaction, employee satisfaction

> **KEY CONCEPT**
>
> The superior performance of any business depends on its general business performance, customer satisfaction, employee satisfaction and the impact it has on society.

and the impact it has on society. The way these are achieved depends on the processes a business has in place, the way it manages its

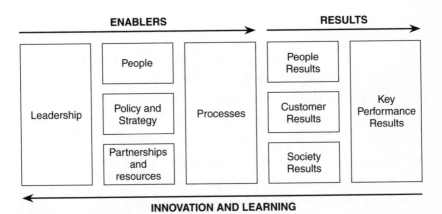

Figure 8.1 *Business Excellence Model.*
Reproduced by permission of the European Foundation for Quality Management

people, the way it uses its resources, the way it formulates strategy and policy and its leadership.

These 'enablers' can be used to represent the intangible assets of an organisation and they can be measured to assess organisational performance. What is being proposed, however, are the dimensions that can be measured under each 'enabler' to see if the organisation is fit to become knowledge-driven organisation. *These dimensions are not proposed by the European Foundation for Quality Management but rather by the author.*

Ten dimensions are presented under each 'enabler' to assess intangible assets without tears. We can take these ten dimensions and ask employees to assess that factor on a scale of 1–5, with 1 being very poor and 5 being excellent.

Such a measurement benchmarked against these dimensions will reflect a gap that can then be attended to if the organisation wants to be the best in class and a genuinely knowledge-driven organisation. The gap will indicate the way this intangible asset is being used to promote knowledge management within the organisation.

A score of 50 points will indicate that the organisation is 'fit for the future' and that it is well-suited to become knowledge driven.

30 points and below will indicate that the organisation has a long way to go to become 'fit for the future'. It has to think very seriously of closing the gaps in order to become a knowledge-driven organisation.

Leadership

Leadership is one of the key intangible assets. Without effective leadership it is not possible for an organisation to transform itself into a knowledge-driven organisation.

In Chapter 6 we defined managing knowledge as the creation of an organisational environment within which information flows smoothly and employees share their experience and knowledge to create organisational knowledge. For such an environment to come into existence, a leader has to pay attention to the following:

> **KEY CONCEPT**
>
> Leadership is one of the key intangible assets.

- The way he/she inspires and motivates staff.
- The way he/she recognises and rewards staff.
- The way he/she promotes knowledge management.
- The way he/she manages his/her team.
- The way he/she involves himself/herself with customers, employees, suppliers and other partners.
- The way he/she communicates strategy and policy.
- The way he/she leads by example.
- The way he/she supports staff development.
- The way he/she makes efforts to institutionalise trust throughout the organisation.
- The way he/she invests in technology to enable knowledge sharing and transfer.

People

People is the second 'enabler' of the Business Excellence Model. The following dimensions can indicate the way people are managed. Does the organisation do the following?

- Undertake training and skill analyses.
- Prepare a skills databank.
- Update the skills databank.
- Develop and sustain the skills and capabilities of its staff.
- Measure staff performance.
- Involve staff in formulating performance objectives.
- Empower its staff.
- Align organisational and staff objectives.
- Promote awareness of health and safety at work.
- Encourage open communication in the organisation.

Policy and strategy

- Does the organisation involve key staff in formulating strategy?
- Is everyone aware of the way strategy is formulated?
- Does the organisation take account of external environmental changes?

- Does the organisation undertake impact analysis of these external changes?
- Is the organisation aware of its strengths, weaknesses, opportunities and threats?
- Is strategy communicated to everyone in the organisation?
- Are strategic objectives aligned with departmental/divisional/team objectives?
- Are strategic objectives aligned with staff performance objectives?
- Does the strategy incorporate providing service excellence to its customers?
- Does the strategy incorporate satisfying staff needs?

Partnerships and resources

- How does the organisation manage its resources in general?
- How does it manage its financial resources?
- How does it manage its cash flow?
- How does it manage its marketing resources?
- How does it manage its IT resources?
- Does it invest adequately in IT to enable it to share and transfer knowledge?
- How does it deal with its suppliers/distributors?
- Does it share communication with its partners?
- How does it manage its tangible assets, such as buildings, equipment and machinery?
- Does the organisation manage its knowledge?

Processes

- Does the organisation manage its customer relationship process adequately?
- Does the organisation manage its production processes adequately?
- Does the organisation manage its staff assessment process adequately?
- Do processes add value for end users?
- Are activities within each process monitored and audited to eliminate non-added-value activities?

- Do processes focus on sharing information within the organisation and with business partners?
- Are processes designed to satisfy customers as end users?
- Does the organisation have a process of listening to its customers?
- Does the organisation have a process of listening to its employees?
- Does innovation play any part in improving key organisational processes?

Results

Organisations can measure the results of how enablers are used in the following areas:

- People satisfaction.
- Customer satisfaction.
- Business results.

Many organisations are conversant with the Business Excellence Model for improving the quality of their products and services. They can, therefore, easily use it to focus on measuring their intangible assets along the lines suggested in order to use and leverage knowledge.

Benchmarking, as we have seen, is about adopting and adapting best practice. This model can be adapted to suit the nature of the organisation and can constitute a model against which organisations can benchmark along the key enablers of superior performance.

Systematic, an independent Danish software house with subsidiaries in the UK and US, has adapted the Business Excellence Model to measure its intangible assets. It assesses the following goals against the model:

Financial goals

1 Increase turnover by specific percentage annually.
2 Maintain net profit ratio of at least 10%.
3 Research and development costs of at least 90% of turnover.

Customer and product goals

1 Increase customer base by two or three new strategic customers per year.
2 Increase turnover of non-defence project customers.
3 Be perceived as a world leading supplier of products for inter-operability between defence organisations and a leading supplier of products for electronic data interchange.
4 Maintain customer satisfaction at a minimum level of 4.0 on a scale of 1 to 5.

Human resource goals

1 Maintain a high level of education among employees.
2 Enhance skills through continuous on-the-job challenges.
3 Maintain employee satisfaction at a minimum level of 3.5 on a scale of 1 to 5.

Quality and process goals

1 Be among the top quality software companies.
2 Improve performance in the software development process by specific set targets.
3 Implement a system for efficient knowledge management.

The business objectives are measured under the categories of customers, employees, processes, infrastructures (supporting the business processes), innovation, external relationships and knowledge management.

Balanced Scorecard

The Balanced Scorecard approach was proposed by Robert Kaplan, professor of accounting at Harvard Business School, and David Norton, president of Renaissance Strategy Group, a consulting firm.

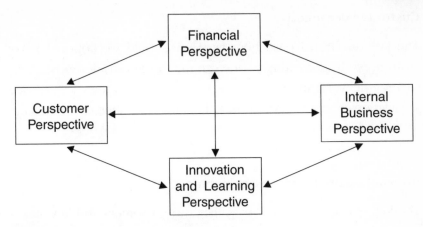

Figure 8.2 *Balanced Scorecard.*

The advantage of adopting a Balanced Scorecard is its comprehensiveness in measuring various key dimensions of business and the way it translates corporate strategic objectives into a coherent set of performance measures.

The method focuses on four dimensions of business: financial performance, customer performance, internal processes and innovation and learning. By selecting a limited number of critical indicators under each perspective, the scorecard helps focus the strategic vision.

The benefit of this method is that it attempts to integrate the measurement of tangible as well as intangible assets.

Financial perspective

Under this category an organisation can formulate financial performance indicators that are appropriate and relevant to its business.

For example, one can measure return on capital employed, operating expenses, cash flow, project profitability, liquidity, solvency, revenue growth etc.

The key question asked here is, 'To succeed financially, how should we appear to our shareholders or stakeholders?''

You can then come up with specific measures to monitor your progress and subsequently your achievements in the area.

Customer perspective

The key question to ask here is, 'How should we appear to our customers?' In this category one can measure customer satisfaction survey, delivery time, customer care index, after-sales service satisfaction, market share, repeat business, number of complaints received and so on.

Internal business processes perspective

The key question here is, 'To satisfy our customers and key stakeholders, what business processes must we excel at?' One could measure tender success rate, project performance index, project close-out cycle, hours spent with new customers on a new project or assignment, safety incident index, speed of fulfilment, time to market and so on.

Innovation and learning perspective

The key question to focus on is, 'How do we sustain our ability to change and to remain fit for the future?' The measures here could include attrition rate, staff attitude survey, Investor in People certification, training days per year, per cent change of revenue from new products, knowledge sharing and so on

Coming up with critical performance measures under each category will cover the measurement of intangible assets. The essence of the Balanced Scorecard is to capture corporate strategy in measurement. If your corporate strategy is to become a knowledge-driven organisation, for example, then your measures should be directed towards processes that facilitate managing knowledge and how the organisation builds knowledge on customers, employees, external relationships, the environment within which it operates and their impact on business results.

Case Study: Introducing a Balanced Scorecard approach

Focus, a publishing company, was established more than 75 years ago by a Scottish entrepreneur and it has since grown into a very reputable company. It publishes numerous journals and magazines. A wide range of advertisers round the world advertise in its magazines where its target audience can reliably be found. Outperforming the competition is Focus's main goal and the strength of its reputation and the competencies of its staff make this possible. It consistently produces superior results.

The company consists of distinct businesses, namely an academic journals division, a social journals division, a books division and an events planning division.

The company has been getting its infrastructure in place to match the size of the business now and to provide a spring-board for future growth. The financial system of the company is provided by Moneysoft, and the teams have been working hard on the first step to implement changes in the financial reporting and budgetary systems. The first element went live as planned in January 2000. The roll-out throughout the business divisions continued throughout the 2000–2001 period. This is a major investment and commitment to company-wide information that will give the group more tools with which to manage an increasingly complex business.

The company has decided to adopt the Balanced Scorecard approach as it has come to realise that the key intangible asset driving its business is knowledge, consisting of the talent of its staff and customers. The adoption of the Balanced Scorecard will measure the creation of value by distinct businesses for existing and future customers and it will incorporate internal capabilities and people competencies in order to enhance the company's future performance.

The Balanced Scorecard provides an effective framework of measurement and categorisation. Also in constructing any

CONTINUED ... Case Study: Introducing a Balanced Scorecard approach

measurement of intellectual capital the process of developing an intellectual capital language becomes very important. The process of developing a language involves identifying areas of concern.

Focus identified the following areas of concern:

- Enhancing financial performance.
- Understanding customers and their needs.
- Developing its customer base.
- The ability to develop and renew its diverse products and services.
- Development of staff to update their competencies.
- Maintaining and developing key processes to develop its business results.
- Building and sustaining the reputation of the company.
- Getting all editors to work as a team and share their knowledge.

These areas of concern reflect the company's assets, including processes that need to be understood in order for the company to gain and sustain competitive advantage.

The company decided to categorise its concerns within the framework of the Balanced Scorecard. It began by identifying intellectual assets, resources and capabilities.

Financial perspective

Indicators will include company turnover, divisional turnover, operating profit, profit per division, profit per group of publications, profit per region.

Customer perspective

Number of customers, size of customer base, growth of customer base, repeat business, customer satisfaction, customer

CONTINUED . . . Case Study: Introducing a Balanced Scorecard approach

relationship (number of visits made to key customers), customer loyalty.

Process perspective

Speed of fulfilment process (from order to delivery), value-adding activities, knowledge transfer and acquisition process, new product development/innovation rate, speed of information, staff performance measurement, the way complaints are received and attended to.

Learning and growth perspective

Number of employees, their skills portfolios, identification of skill gaps, skill renewal and development, employee satisfaction, recruitment and retention rates, reputation management.

The above indicators were suggested as 'starters' by the group asked to look into the introduction of the Balanced Scorecard approach.

The first step in adopting such a method was to get commitment from top management. Without such a commitment the project will not be adopted. After that the focus was on getting the rest of the staff to understand the importance of this approach and what it entailed. It was very hard work to get all the staff at each business unit to think of appropriate performance indicators that made sense to them and to the business. Coming up with indicators to measure financial performance was not a problem; the challenge was to come up with meaningful indicators related to customers, processes and learning.

Focus decided to tackle the measurement of intangible assets at a strategic level. The board formulated a mission

> **CONTINUED ... Case Study: Introducing a Balanced Scorecard approach**
>
> statement that reflected measuring and enhancing intangible assets.
>
> The process the company went through to adopt the Balanced Scorecard approach was as follows:
>
> - Identify its areas of business concern.
> - Identify the method that will address these concerns.
> - Decided that the Balanced Scorecard was an appropriate method for them to use.
> - All staff were informed of top management's decision to adopt this method and the reasons for doing so.
> - All senior managers received information on the nature of the Balanced Scorecard.
> - Each business unit had to form a team that would come up with meaningful and appropriate indicators under each perspective.
> - All staff were encouraged to contribute.
> - A facilitator was appointed to review and assess the results.
> - The board met to fine-tune the process and to come up with an action plan.
> - The implementation plan was prepared and implemented.
> - 'Hiccups' were recorded and monitored and actions taken to eliminate them.

Skandia Navigator

The third method of measuring intangible assets is known as the Skandia Navigator.

The navigator is a tool for measuring intellectual capital devised by Skandia AFS, a Swedish financial services company. Skandia decided that it was important to assess and measure intellectual capital as it was one of the key drivers of business growth and an engine of

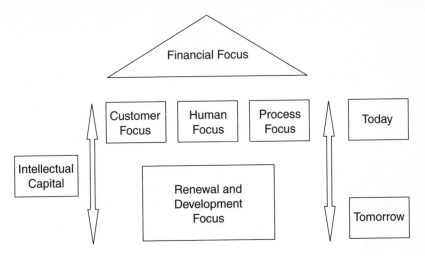

Figure 8.3   *Skandia Navigator.*

innovation. It defined intellectual capital as human capital plus structural capital.

Human capital was their staff. Structural capital was represented by such things as the customer database, IT systems, processes and intellectual property. The focus of measurement was to develop and renew both human and structural capital.

The Navigator measures human and structural capital as they are today in relation to their growth in the future to meet company's strategic objectives.

Intangible Assets Monitor

This method was devised by Dr Karl Erik Sveiby, a consultant and leading author on knowledge-based assets. According to Dr Sveiby, the intangible assets of an organisation consist of family of three, namely external structure, internal structure and employee competence.

External structure includes relationship with customers and suppliers, brand names, trade marks and reputation. This category also includes relationship with collaborators and other business partners.

Internal structure consists of patents, concepts, models, and computer and administrative systems that are part of the organisation.

Employee competence refers to the capacity to act in a wide variety of situations. It includes staff's attitude, skills, experience and energy.

The three structures are inter-related. The performance indicators under each structure are focused on growth, efficiency and stability.

Dr Sveiby claims that creating value by leveraging intangible assets is what managing knowledge is all about: 'To be able to do that, you have to visualise your organisation as consisting of nothing but knowledge and knowledge flows.' Since intangible assets are important, every opportunity should be taken by the business to enhance and leverage these assets.

A company that has used this method effectively is Celemi. The following article, written by the President of Celemi, raises key questions regarding measuring intangible assets.

Growing a knowledge company: answers to frequently asked questions about measuring and managing intangible assets

Margareta Barchan, Celemi's President & CEO

Leaders of knowledge companies are beginning to take a closer look at the financial indicators that affect their operations, and they are finding a new set of criteria emerging: the value of their intangible assets. These new financial guidelines are challenging the usefulness of tracking only traditional performance measures typically found in the company's balance sheet.

Intangible assets include the ability to attract and retain image-enhancing clients or customers as well as skilled employees. Innovation, reputation and know-how are all integral components in a knowledge company that should be measured and managed in order to achieve the best performance. Knowledge-based organizations include consulting firms, financial institutions, law firms, software developers and advertising agencies – any organization in which profitability depends on providing a unique, effective solution to clients every time. But organizations like these do not have a monopoly on knowledge.

Even traditional manufacturing companies with operations that invest heavily in research and development can be knowledge-driven. Such organizations include pharmaceutical, high-tech and chemical companies.

So, what does it take to capitalize on knowledge and help your organization grow? As the chief executive of a company that develops learning processes for improved business performance, and who has been monitoring the company's intangible assets for the last two years, I'd like to share with you my responses to questions I am frequently asked about my experiences in knowledge management.

'The investments we are making today in our organization's internal structure, the competence of our people, and attracting and retaining the right clients is a well-planned strategy to increase our profitability in the future.'

Q. **Why did Celemi decide to measure and manage its intangible assets?**

A. 'As a developer of learning processes, we had been involved in the creation of a new simulation that we call Tango, which helps people identify the key intangible assets in their own company. Tango participants discover how to measure these assets and how to manage them in coordination with the standard tangible assets. As we worked on this simulation internally, we began naturally to adopt some of the terminology and methodology for ourselves, as we are a typical knowledge-based company. In 1994, at the same time we introduced Tango to the market, our board of directors made the decision to formally adopt this approach, and we reported our first intangible assets figures in our 1995 annual report.'

Q. **To report your intangible assets, you have developed a special matrix or 'monitor.' How did you determine which categories to include?**

A. 'We took the advice of business consultant Dr. Karl Erik Sveiby, a member of our product advisory board, who has been studying intangible assets for more than 15 years. We started with the basics – how many clients do we have? What types of clients do we have? Do they enhance our image? Then, we looked directly at the knowledge value of our company. This is broken into two distinct categories. First, the knowledge owned by our company; our research and development and innovative learning products that can be adapted and reproduced for our clients. But we are also concerned with the individual knowledge of each person who is working in or with Celemi. While we cannot own this knowledge, we can take proactive steps to transfer this knowledge directly into the business by making sure that everyone is working to improve the business in his or her particular niche. And, when people feel challenged and fulfilled they will stay longer. If you want to ensure the growth of your business you must invest in the competence development of your workforce.'

Q. **How do you place value on your intangible assets?**

A. 'We study them from different levels. First, we have growth and renewal. Then we have efficiency and, finally, stability of different parameters in the company.'

Q. **What are the key factors for growth and renewal?**

A. 'We monitor growth and renewal in two areas: the company and the clients. For example, we made large investments in technology in 1994 when we opened several new subsidiaries around the world. While it cost us a substantial amount of money at the time, it also indicated a burst of growth for the company, something we are reaping the benefits of now. But I firmly believe that the most important factor in the growth of our company, or any knowledge company, is the client base. Knowledge companies must realize the full value of their clients. It's not just income. If you are able to attract and retain the right clients, you automatically increase the knowledge base of your company. Here's why: when you take on a client with a challenging or new assignment and you complete it successfully, your company has gained image value, your employees have developed a new competence or skill, and your business now has a new solution that it owns which may be adaptable to other clients' situations. One of the greatest benefits of monitoring our intangible assets is that it has helped us identify who these "right" clients are.'

Q. **How are these measures linked to your overall corporate strategy?**

A. 'We use these measures to make sure that the company is on course, moving in the right direction. In addition, we can attach a concrete number to these intangible assets to help our own employees understand our overall business strategy. Right now, we value the awareness that these factors bring more than the specific figures they represent.'

Q. **In a few areas, your intangible assets figures this year do not appear to be as strong as they had been in the past. Does this concern you? And, does it change the way you will manage the business?**

A. 'Some of the figures indicate areas that need to be taken care of. But other areas are negatively affected by design. For example, a large number of newly employed people could be a sign of instability in a company and shows up as a weak rating on the Intangible Assets Monitor. However, we did not hire new people to replace people who left, we hired new people because our business is growing so fast. You will also notice that our "rookie ratio" has been high in the past. This is the percentage of new employees in relation to long-term employees and it takes into account skills and seniority. Generally you want to have a low rookie ratio. However, it is part of our strategy to hire young, qualified people because we want to invest in training them and developing their skills according to our corporate values and philosophy. This figure will improve over time as they develop competence and seniority. I have no problem with intangible assets ratings that indicate areas of weakness as long as I know that the figure is a direct result of our strategy, and that we are in control of these areas, and that they will improve. And that is the point. It is not so much the value of the number as it is the understanding of what is driving the future performance of the company.'

Q. **Do you use these measures to evaluate and reward people?**

A. 'Not individually. No. The focus now is to monitor these figures on the overall strategic level of our global company. But I can use these figures to track issues and trends at the operational level – for the individual offices in the U.S., Sweden, the U.K. and Belgium and Finland. For example, I can use the intangible assets information we monitor to let a general manager know that his or her office needs to attract a certain type of client to enhance the overall image of our company. But I cannot use these figures to say to an individual that he or she is personally doing a good job. I would say that being aware of the intangible assets provides general guidelines to employees that help them understand where the focus of their jobs should be.'

Q. **Has measuring your intangible assets had any impact on your financial performance?**

A. 'It probably has, but that is not our concern right now. We look at our investments in intangible assets as a long-term strategy that will pay off later. The investments we are making today in our organization's internal structure, the competence of our people, and attracting and retaining the right clients are part of a well-planned strategy to increase our profitability in the future. Even though we are new at this and are making some large investments up front, I am still very pleased with our financial performance. While the balance sheet indicates a reduced profit, which is directly related to the investments in our intangible assets, we continue to enjoy a healthy growth in sales.'

Q. **What advice would you give to business leaders who are beginning to think about the role intangible assets play in their organizations?**

A. 'Don't just jump in and start measuring your intangible assets. First, create an understanding internally of what intangible assets are and what they mean to the overall performance of your company. Everyone needs to understand the role of intangible assets in order to change their own performance. Without internal buy-in, it doesn't matter whether you measure your intangibles or not – no positive changes will be made. Also, don't select intangible assets categories indiscriminately or just because that's what someone else is measuring. Start with an assessment of your company's big picture, and make sure everyone shares this vision. Then you can step back and determine which intangible assets are the most applicable to your business operation.'

Margareta Barchan (President and CEO of Celemiab), 1997. Reproduced by permission of Celemiab International AB. All rights reserved.

Customise Your Method

If your business does not want to use any of the 'off-the-shelf' methods then you can design your own intangible assets measurement method, provided that you consider the following:

- The objectives of the measurement – why do you want to measure in the first place?
- What is it that you want to measure?
- Involve all assets, tangible and intangible, in your measurement method.
- Come up with meaningful and appropriate indicators.
- Involve all staff in formulating measurement indicators.
- Categorise assets as suits your business.
- The method of measurement should add value.
- What are the desired outcomes?
- What actions are you going to take to assess the outcomes?
- What process have you in place to close the gaps?

Continuous Improvement

The performance of any business should be monitored continuously. Once an organisation has decided on performance objectives, these objectives should be monitored continuously to find out if the organisation is on the right track and it is achieving its objectives within the time limits set. If not, then adjustments have to be made to get it back on track.

Information gathered and decisions taken should be recorded to create explicit knowledge that people can use to monitor progress and make necessary decisions. The PDCA cycle (see Figure 1.1) should be applied to preparing a skills audit, assessing the value-adding aspects of business, monitoring staff performance, assessing customers' needs, promoting innovation and collecting information on competition and competitors. In fact, it should be applied to key business drivers to capture change and create knowledge.

> **KEY CONCEPT**
>
> The performance of any organisation should be monitored continuously.

Valuing Brands

As we saw in Chapter 7, some organisations have brands that constitute intangible assets. There are corporate brands such as IBM, Dell, ICI, Microsoft and Shell and there are product brands.

Brands generally reflect corporate values and they create certain images in customers' and consumers' minds. A powerful brand has a high brand equity, to the extent that it has strong brand loyalty and is a very valuable intangible asset.

To have an established and reputable brand is an onerous task in that it has to be constantly managed. A brand is also a powerful tool that enables an organisation to differentiate itself from its key competitors.

Just as an employee joins an organisation with a psychological contract in mind, with the brand there is a 'contract' between customer and organisation, which could be an emotional/psychological contract. This provides security for the company and this is what the experts debate when they consider valuing brands.

There are some specialised organisations such as Interbrand that specialise in brand valuation. The value of brands plays a key role in acquisitions, for example. This was evidenced when Nestlé acquired Rowntree and when Grand Metropolitan acquired Pilsbury. In many cases the price being paid for the acquisition is significantly higher than the book value of the tangible assets. It was reported, for instance, that 88% of the price that Grand Metropolitan paid for Pilsbury consisted of payment for the brand name.

Volkswagen bought the assets of the Rolls-Royce automobile corporation for $780 million, but it did not include the brand in the deal. BMW purchased the right to use the Rolls-Royce trademark for $65 million.

A brand enhances organisational capability and its power increases as the organisation achieves superior performance.

Conclusion

Intangible assets are very important for all types and sizes of organisation. Their use enhances organisational capability and enable the organisation to attain high performance.

In this chapter we have highlighted only a few methods that organisations can use to measure and track the performance of their intangible assets.

NINE

Knowledge
Management in
Practice: Making a Start

I hear and I forget, I see and I remember, I do and I understand. (Chinese proverb)

Overview

- This chapter deals with organisations that have adopted best practice in relation to knowledge management.
- Three organisations, one global, one international subsidiary and one UK company, show how they have adopted best practice in the areas of knowledge sharing and managing people.
- Three approaches are advocated to assess your organisational readiness to become a knowledge-driven company.

To make a start on becominge knowledge driven, organisations have to investigate and study best practice. They need to take on board things that can work well in their organisation and refine and change things that may have worked well elsewhere, but for a variety of reasons will not be able to work in their organisation.

Best Practice Approach

There are numerous companies that have adopted effective processes to create and transfer knowledge within their organisations.

Such organisations include BP Amoco, Shell, Chevron, Xerox, the UK Royal Mail, Ernst & Young, McKinsey and so on.

We will focus on three diverse companies to give a feel for the initiatives they have taken to transfer knowledge and manage people for best advantage.

Global company perspective

Case Study: Xerox creates a knowledge-sharing culture through grassroots efforts

By Vicki J. Powers

Xerox Corporation established its identity in the late 1980s as 'The Document Company'. By following this business strategy, it's not surprising the organisation became involved in knowledge management right from the start. Dan Holtshouse, director, Corporate Strategy, says the organization had a hunch – by looking at the growing knowledge management movement in 1995 – that knowledge management would be a natural extension of document management. By acting on this hunch, Xerox developed a knowledge management initiative that impacts the organisation's business strategy and improves its customer service and financial performance.

'If knowledge management was going to prove valid and powerful, we wanted to be an early and effective market leader,' Holtshouse remarks.

A critical beginning

Before Xerox could commit to knowledge management, Holtshouse says, the organization needed to understand its customers' and the marketplace's knowledge interest. To determine this, Xerox took an across-the-board look at the subject – the underlying interests, drivers and implications to the company.

CONTINUED ... Case Study: Xerox creates a knowledge-sharing culture through grassroots efforts

Xerox interviewed 60 knowledge workers outside the organization to research the productivity of knowledge work. Holtshouse realized that organizations use and equate knowledge management in a number of ways, depending on their culture. Yet almost every organization, he found, uses knowledge management for knowledge sharing or the transfer of best practices.

Based on significant research and study participation with Ernst & Young, the American Productivity & Quality Centre, and Boston University, Xerox built a library of case studies describing the knowledge activities of other organizations. Holtshouse analyzed the activities that organizations associate with knowledge management and divided them into 10 distinct areas – or 10 domains of knowledge management. These domains are:

- Sharing knowledge and best practices.
- Instilling responsibility for knowledge sharing.
- Capturing and reusing past experiences.
- Embedding knowledge in products, services, and processes.
- Producing knowledge as a product.
- Driving knowledge generation for innovation.
- Mapping networks of experts.
- Building and mining customer knowledge bases.
- Understanding and measuring the value of knowledge.
- Leveraging intellectual assets.

Holtshouse says the 10 domains were useful in helping Xerox employees quickly understand 'this thing' called knowledge management. He believes it was fundamental to getting alignment in thinking on what constitutes this often-confusing term.

CONTINUED ... Case Study: Xerox creates a knowledge-sharing culture through grassroots efforts

'Over time, I found that to get a shared vision of the importance of knowledge management, you had to address what the three or four conflicting ideas might be around knowledge management inside a company,' Holtshouse relates. 'We had to develop explicit contrasts on how knowledge management is different from information management or how a team or work group is different from a community. By building those representations, we were able to help shape the shared thinking of what knowledge management is.'

Holtshouse admits it was a reasonable amount of work to synthesize the main knowledge management activities at the different organizations. Some organizations had two or three initiatives under way in knowledge management while other organizations had a total focus around one area. Chevron, for example, focuses mainly on sharing best practices.

'I would say Xerox has activities in most of the domains,' Holtshouse says. 'I have a map of internal projects, and we're active in seven of the 10. We have activities in the other three, but they don't have the visibility of the ones that fall in the seven. We believe those domains represent the framework of the knowledge-driven organization of the future. We believe that most companies that want to consider themselves knowledge-based or a knowledge company will need to master all 10.'

Support for knowledge

As a part of its knowledge work study, Xerox recruited 100 knowledge managers in 1997 who were directly involved in leading knowledge initiatives in the United States and Europe. This panel of experts – who were challenging to find at that

CONTINUED . . . Case Study: Xerox creates a knowledge-sharing culture through grassroots efforts

time – agreed to be surveyed each year regarding their knowledge management initiatives and developing trends. The main benefit of the knowledge panel, explains Holtshouse, is that the membership represents the bigger part of the movement.

'The people who are written about for best practices or those who win awards are the leading-edge companies,' Holtshouse says. 'But what about the companies that are not on the leading edge? We think they are couple of years behind. The knowledge panel is helping us get a feel for where the bigger part of the group is. These people are the ones trying to develop the systems, but they might not have the top management support yet.'

Xerox, fortunately, has had that support from the beginning. Its chairman, Paul Allaire, officially kicked off the organization's knowledge management initiative in 1996. In the same year Xerox began a major, long-range planning effort dubbed Xerox 2005. This process helped the company examine its future – where technology was going, where consumers were going, and what geographies were changing – and make midcourse corrections where necessary. Holtshouse's knowledge management study conducted in 1996 served as input to this long-range planning effort.

Xerox's knowledge in action

Holtshouse says Xerox has consciously set out to be as educated as possible about knowledge management. The organization has spent considerable resources and time to understand the collective knowledge around the subject through its finished research, consortium work, and sponsorship of research.

CONTINUED ... Case Study: Xerox creates a knowledge-sharing culture through grassroots efforts

Xerox boasts many examples of how knowledge sharing has worked within the organization. It developed a number grass-roots initiatives to help solve specific problems. Xerox also created several corporate initiatives that combine what the organization is doing and what it is learning within its own walls.

Eureka

Eureka is a grassroots effort that started from a business necessity to share intellectual capital. This knowledge base allows Xerox's service organization to create and reuse intellectual capital among its 25 000 reps worldwide.

Xerox service technicians make approximately 1 million service calls per month to maintain copiers, printers and networks. During these repairs, employees sometimes discovered problems they had not seen in documentation. It might relate to a new part, a vendor problem, or an out-of-date service manual. These problems could create a lengthy downtime for customers. At the same time, Xerox could lose money as service reps worked to solve a challenging problem.

'Eureka was developed so once somebody spends a lot of time developing this expensive answer, it gets shared, and other employees don't have to repeat it,' Holtshouse states. 'Customers get better service because when it occurs again, someone else doesn't have to spend that much time on it. It's also a significant cost reduction opportunity and encourages high involvement in the service organization as reps create the knowledge base and use it.'

Eureka, Holtshouse explains, is self-sustaining. Service reps, rather than outside reporters or writers, contribute their innovative solutions to the knowledge base on their own time.

CONTINUED ... Case Study: Xerox creates a knowledge-sharing culture through grassroots efforts

Currently, the knowledge sharing system has more than 25 000 records. To access this knowledge-sharing environment, reps use their laptops and enter the specific problem that needs to be fixed at the client's site and receive suggested solutions submitted by other Xerox employees. Before, Eureka, service reps shared their innovative solutions in work group meetings, but the sharing was limited to only a few people at a time.

'The voluntary submission of those shared tips, we think, is due primarily to the service reps getting personal recognition for their contributions, because their name goes with the tip throughout the life of the system,' Holtshouse reports.

In addition to developing intellectual capital, Eureka contributes to the social capital because employees are beginning to know each other beyond their immediate work groups. Service reps within a geographic area generally work in teams of eight to 10 employees and communicate by radio phone and e-mail. Eureka has allowed service reps to become part of a worldwide global community. A solution developed in Toronto, for example, was used by someone in South America. Holtshouse says the employee e-mailed across the globe to the other employee that his solution was terrific. 'You saved me from replacing a $40 000 machine by simply replacing this 9-cent connector. I would never have figured it out.'

Xerox currently saves between 5 percent and 10 percent on labor and parts costs from the success of its Eureka project. With a 25 000-person labor organization, Holtshouse says, that's a lot of money. Plus, employees are naturally working hard to reduce costs to support customer anyway. Altogether, the savings total tens of millions of dollars, Holtshouse reports.

A number of groups within Xerox are interested in the experience that Eureka has created in the service community

CONTINUED ... Case Study: Xerox creates a knowledge-sharing culture through grassroots efforts

and want to apply that methodology and process to other communities in the organization. The help desk, for example, is using the knowledge base for call center support. But while Xerox has been talking with a few customers outside the organization that might benefit from a Eureka-like system in their service organization, Eureka is only an internal Xerox solution at this point.

DocuShare

Xerox's research lab community developed its own Web-based tool to share progress with other scientists working on the same project. These scientists need little structure and wanted to be able to self-maintain and self-organize their workspaces. Holtshouse says Xerox was cautious about just putting some technology in place because it wouldn't get used unless it matched the motivations of the community. The resulting tool, first called AmberWeb and now DocuShare, allows scientists to collaborate among themselves. It has also moved outside the science arena, where scientists are working with engineers and product designers share business planners and marketers. The community using DocuShare has grown from 500 research engineers to 30 000 employees inside Xerox.

'The interesting part about Eureka and DocuShare is that we sent a team of scientists to work beside the employees to understand what would motivate them to use these tools,' Holtshouse explains. 'They brought with them a lot of behavioural science, anthropological eyeglasses to understand how the employees work. If you are careful in addressing the cultural work practice of a community, that will ensure a higher success rate in developing the right knowledge solution.'

CONTINUED ... Case Study: Xerox creates a knowledge-sharing culture through grassroots efforts

Evolving challenges

The challenge of establishing a knowledge management effort at Xerox has changed over time, according to Holtshouse. He explains the first year involved putting aside the concern that the effort might be a waste of time, because no one knew how important knowledge management was going to be.

'It was like a lot that are new – you just don't know,' Holtshouse relates. 'Even though you have support from the top, you have to work through a lot of barriers from employees who don't have the same perspective around this new thing called knowledge management.'

Later the challenge transitioned to building a community and pulling together community sharing around knowledge management with the working champions inside the company. It also meant working with other Xerox businesses and research labs to receive a commitment to focus on this. Holtshouse says competing themes or business opportunities always exist, so focusing on knowledge management meant taking time and resources away from other proprieties.

The future of knowledge sharing at Xerox

Eureka and DocuShare represent large community knowledge-sharing initiatives of 25 000 or more employees. The next goal for Xerox is to encourage knowledge sharing among all 90 000 employees as part of their everyday work. To keep the knowledge momentum building across the entire Xerox community, a new cultural dimension is being launched in 2000 around knowledge sharing so that it becomes a part of everyone's daily activities, whether or not they have direct involvement with a special initiative such as Eureka or DocuShare.

CONTINUED ... Case Study: Xerox creates a knowledge-sharing culture through grassroots efforts

Xerox – lessons learned

Contrast for employees the difference between knowledge management and the way they used to work.

Don't take for granted everyone understands what you're trying to build or accomplish. 'Try to come at it in a number of ways so people understand the perspective that you are talking about,' Holtshouse notes.

Support from the top is vital in a change initiative, and knowledge management is all about change.

Getting people to want to participate in knowledge management is easy; getting them to do it right takes more effort. 'We had a lot of people wanting to join in with knowledge management but not to do anything differently so they would rename what they were doing "knowledge this and knowledge that,"' Holtshouse says. 'That required another iteration of communications through a knowledge newsletter and a better Web site to help align collective thinking across the organization.'

Vicki J. Powers, Xerox Creates a Knowledge-Sharing Culture Through Grassroots Efforts. *APQC Knowledge Management in Practice*, Fourth Quarter 1999. Reproduced by permission of the American Productivity & Quality Center.

A subsidiary company perspective

Case study: Yamazaki UK Ltd

Yamazaki Machinery UK Ltd (YMUK) is a wholly owned subsidiary of the international Yamazaki–Mazak organisation, a Japanese corporation and one of the largest machine tool manufacturers in the world. YMUK designs and manufactures

CONTINUED . . . Case study: Yamazaki UK Ltd

computer-controlled machine tools under the name Mazak Machine Tools and employs 420 people at its plant in Worcester and 200 in the rest of Europe.

In 1987, the Yamazaki–Mazak Corporation opened its new state-of-the-art European factory in Worcester. The management of this showpiece plant faced the challenge of establishing a new company to match the Japanese standards of excellence in an industry that was in decline in the UK.

The new YMUK management team, recognising that the key to success was in its employees, made a significant investment in the recruitment process. Careful analysis identified the skills, abilities and attitudes that were required by the company.

Analysis of the labour market showed what skills were available and recruitment profiles were used to guide a rigorous staff selection process. The first recruits were trained in Japan and then brought back to train others in the UK.

A range of personnel policies was developed to support a continuous improvement environment:

- Personnel professionals became internal consultants to support managers in the development of people.
- An appraisal system was linked to performance-related pay and was used to create individual development plans and learning contracts.
- Managers were assessed on the quality of development plans created for their people.

New staff received a formal induction programme followed by a six-month appraisal and there were regular reviews of development plans, learning contracts and development actions. All staff were trained in basic problem-solving techniques.

These policies were supported by systems designed to ensure good communication and teamwork, including:

CONTINUED ... Case study: Yamazaki UK Ltd

- Daily team briefings and monthly plant meetings.
- A staff council and a regular news-sheet.
- Visible indicators to emphasise the common conditions culture – open-plan layouts, single-status workwear in production, equal access to car parks, changing rooms and the restaurant.
- Measurement criteria for individual performance included 'team contribution'.
- Total Quality Control groups were based around work teams.

In late 1991, YMUK approached HAWTEC for information on Investors in People. The company made no immediate formal commitment but compiled a portfolio of evidence in order to compare company practices with the Investors in People Standards. On the basis of this evidence, HAWTEC recommended that YMUK apply for formal assessment.

YMUK has achieved its objective of establishing Japanese levels of efficiency and effectiveness and has become one of the largest machine tool manufacturers in Europe. The company is no longer dependent on Japan for systems design and development engineering.

In four years, production was built from zero to 100 machine tools per month, 80–85% of which were exported. The company succeeded in reaching its performance targets even during the reduced activity of the recession.

The company has kept pace with the rapidly rising expectations of customers. Delivery schedules are achieved despite changing market requirements. The workforce participates in continuous improvement and has the ability to handle the demands of new technology.

The excellence of the company has been recognised in the following ways:

CONTINUED ... Case study: Yamazaki UK Ltd

- No. 1 UK Manufacturer – *Management Today* survey, 1989.
- 'Best in World' – Swedish Academy of Engineering Science, 1991.
- Queen's Award for Export Achievement, 1992.
- BS5750/ISO 9000, 1992.
- Investor in People.

YMUK was recognised as an Investor in People by HAWTEC in 1993 and was reaccredited in 1996. Investors in People provided a framework within which YMUK could audit its actions, assess the level of achievement and the amount of progress towards its goals. The reassessment process was useful in allowing the company to estimate the extent to which it had achieved constant improvement in the management of its most important asset – people.

It was particularly useful to monitor how the company's people management policies had responded to changes in the organisation: new senior managers, an increased and maturing workforce, plant expansion and changes in production.

Reproduced by permission of Investors in People UK.

A UK company perspective

Case study: Ideas into action – Strachan & Henshaw generate profitable ideas

Specialist engineering company Strachan & Henshaw Ltd, has discovered an excellent method of generating profitable ideas and, more importantly, found ways to drive these through to action.

Senior project engineer Roger Taylor believes Inside UK Enterprise (IUKE) assists in meeting the company's objective of increasing productivity and profitability.

**CONTINUED ... Case study: Ideas into action –
Strachan & Henshaw generate profitable ideas**

Strachan & Henshaw personnel first attended a site visit over two years ago, and since then 80 employees have been on approximately 40 visits, including British Airways, Rolls-Royce, Birmingham Midshires and CRL. A further 10 are planned for later this year.

Taylor explains: 'The scheme has already generated a significant number of ideas for our company that will help us to grow and adapt to meet the challenges ahead, for example differing approaches to Business Excellence, use of benchmarking and performance targets, variations of procurement strategy and addressing staff cultural issues.'

He explains that the company sends a wide cross-section of people on the visits: 'The aim is to raise awareness – at all levels – of how other businesses are run. This way, people think of the ideas themselves, rather than having these imposed by others. We then ensure someone drives the project forward. Successful business improvements come from the grass roots.'

'To build a broader awareness of those companies that reflect our aspirations, we have visited organisations such as British Airways, Rolls-Royce, Frederick Woolley Ltd, Sandusky Walmsley Ltd several times in order to build up a thorough picture of how their businesses are supported and developed internally.'

Overall Taylor recommends the opportunity to share best practice: 'Companies should definitely get involved if they are looking to improve.'

Reproduced by permission of Strachan & Henshaw.

Benchmarking

Companies wanting to become knowledge driven can also conduct best practice benchmarking, as described in Chapter 1.

If, however, benchmarking is not feasible for whatever reason, then involve your staff in building your own model of best practice to benchmark against.

> **KEY CONCEPT**
>
> Create your own ideal organisation.

Get your staff together to design along the following proposition: *'What would be your ideal best practice organisation in our business sector?'*

Organisational Audit

A third approach would be to undertake a comprehensive organisational audit to see if the organisation is ready to embark on a knowledge management initiative and what gaps exist and how to close them.

Organisations can do an audit to identify gaps by examining the following:

1 The way they formulate their strategy.
2 The way they recruit and retain their people.
3 The way they manage their people.
4 The nature of their culture.
5 The nature of their leadership.
6 The way they build and maintain relationships with their customers.
7 The way they treat their business partners.
8 The systems they have (assessing rigidity in decision making and communication).

The simple approach is to use a five-point scale to identify gaps. The audit is conducted by doing surveys to establish the gaps.

Employees, customers and other business partners can be asked to respond to questions similar to the following (the exact nature of the questions asked will depend on the business). Participants should be asked to score on a 1–5 scale, where 1 shows a 'very poor' assessment and, 5 shows an 'excellent' assessment.

25 points under each category would indicate that the organisation has no gaps to attend to and it is perfectly positioned to become a learning and a knowledge-driven organisation.

5 points under a particular category would reflect that the organisation has big gap in this category that needs to be attended to.

Strategy

- Do sections of junior employees make any contribution to the formulation of strategy?
- Does the organisation scan the external environment within which it operates?
- Does the organisation undertake strengths/weaknesses/ opportunities/threats analysis?
- Does the organisation continuously monitor its strategy?
- Does the organisation prepare appropriate and adequate performance measures to track its strategic objectives?

Recruitment and retention of staff

- Does the organisation do adequate preparation to identify the skills gap before recruitment?
- Do senior managers take part in recruitment?
- Is there an induction programme for new recruits immediately after recruitment?
- Does the organisation have incentive schemes to retain its staff?
- Does the organisation undertake staff satisfaction surveys at least once a year?

Managing people

- Does the organisation conduct motivational analysis of its staff?
- Does the organisation align its strategic objectives with staff performance objectives?
- Do staff participate fully in preparing their performance objectives?
- Are staff appraised regularly?

- Is the performance appraisal system tied to the staff development programme?

Culture

- Does the culture of the organisation promote collaboration?
- Do staff trust top management?
- Do staff trust each other?
- Is the culture flexible enough to respond to market changes?
- Are there sub-cultures within the overall culture that create rigidity?

Leadership

- Are decisions made in a bureaucratic way?
- Are leaders within the organisation trusted?
- Do leaders coach their staff?
- Do leaders empower their staff?
- Are leaders accessible to their staff?

Customers

- Does the organisation keep information on customers' needs?
- Does the organisation make efforts to listen to customers?
- Does the organisations care about customer loyalty?
- Does the organisation provide service excellence to its customers?
- Does your organisation maintain good relationships with its key customers?

Business partners

- Does the organisation try to build good relationships with its business partners?
- Does the organisation share key information with its partners?
- Does the organisation treat distributors/dealers as true partners?
- Does the organisation make regular contacts with its partners?

- Does the organisation solicit views about its performance from its partners?

Systems/processes

- Do systems facilitate smooth communication within the organisation?
- Do systems facilitate information storage?
- Do processes and systems enable knowledge sharing and transfer?
- Does the organisation review systems and processes continuously?
- Does the organisation have staff review and customer surveys processes in place?

After auditing, make plans to close the gaps and you will be on your way to putting in place processes of knowledge creation and transfer.

Your organisation has to plan to close the gap and the plan should be prepared on SMARTER principles:

S   Be specific as to what is to be achieved.

M   Formulate performance measures to track your objectives.

A   Make sure the targets are achievable.

R   Make sure the targets set are realistic and not too ambitious.

T   Put a time scale on what should be done by when.

E   Empower your staff to facilitate speedy decision making.

R   Record your achievements to capture knowledge.

Be rigorous in your auditing – and good luck.

TEN

A to Z of Managing Knowledge

A

Aspire to become a knowledge-driven organisation.

Achievements of staff should be documented.

Adopt and adapt when you are undertaking a benchmarking exercise.

Align staff objectives with organisational objectives.

Articulate your organisational vision very clearly.

Acquaint yourself with processes of knowledge creation and knowledge transfer.

Advocate a best practice mindset throughout your organisation.

B

Benchmark to adopt best practice.

Brainstorm regularly with your staff to continuously monitor and come up with new ideas.

Barriers to communication should be abolished.

Best practice will become a business imperative.

Be prepared to face business challenges.

C

Communicate openly and honestly.

Collaborate to gain new insight into best practice.

Credibility should be one of the attributes of your leadership.

Customers should be respected.

Customer satisfaction should be measured at regular intervals.

Command-and-control structures of management should be disbanded.

Continuous improvement should be applied to every aspect of your business.

Collaborative culture will facilitate knowledge sharing and creation.

Coach your staff to share their tacit knowledge.

Capture knowledge from your staff, customers, business partners and competitors.

Commit to your vision and your conviction of the importance of managing knowledge.

D

Data should not be confused with knowledge.

Design appropriate systems to assess your staff and to make appropriate information accessible to your staff.

Develop your staff continuously.

Dimensions of knowledge management include people, customers and business partners.

Decide to take action now.

E

Empower your staff.

Employees are your key intangible assets.

External drivers of your business should be monitored continuously.

Energise your staff to deliver innovation.

F

Focus on what you have set out to achieve.

Facilitate knowledge sharing within your organisation.

Functional silos should be abolished.

Familiarise yourself with the methods of knowledge creation and transfer.

G

Goal setting at organisational level should involve all key employees.

Globalisation should be viewed as a challenge.

H

Help your staff whenever necessary.

Hierarchical structures should be abolished.

I

Incentives should be aligned to objectives set.

Information should be used to build organisational knowledge.

Innovate your business continuously.

Intangible assets should be identified and measured.

Internet, intranets and extranets have become great enablers of knowledge sharing and knowledge creation.

Inspire your staff to deliver superior performance

J

Justify your decisions to your staff.

K

Knowledge provides your organisational capability.

Knowledge management involves connecting people with people and people with technology.

L

Leadership should facilitate change without pain.

Learning should be encouraged.

Leverage intangible assets to gain and sustain competitive advantage.

M

Measure the effectiveness of your tangible as well as intangible assets.

Manage knowledge creation and transfer.

Mentoring should be provided to your staff for their development.

Monitor business results continuously.

Motivate your staff to share and create knowledge and to trust each other.

N

New economy will increasingly become the context within which your business will operate.

O

Open communication should be encouraged within your organisation.

Ownership of knowledge management initiatives should be encouraged and promoted.

P

Praise your staff regularly for good performance.

People (staff and customers), products and processes are your key business drivers.

Psychological contracts are a fact of business life.

Pursue best practice whatever and wherever possible.

Q

Quality of thinking and products/services should be the cornerstone of your business.

Quest for knowledge should be encouraged.

Questionnaires should be used to build a knowledge bank in relation to customer needs and skills of employees.

R

Retain your staff.

Recruit carefully.

Recognise your staff for their good performance.

Relationship building within and outside the organisation should be encouraged.

Resources should be transformed into capabilities.

S

Skills should be consistently updated.

Staff constitute your key intangible assets.

Service excellence should be the vision of your organisation.

SMARTER principles should be applied in planning to manage knowledge.

Sociological, technological, economic and political (STEP) factors should be monitored to assess their impact on your business and to build knowledge of external factors.

Strategic objectives should include managing knowledge.

Success of your organisation will depend on the way you manage knowledge and the way you adopt and adapt best practice.

T

Teams should be encouraged to share knowledge.

Technology is the main enabler of knowledge creation and transfer.

Train your staff continuously to update their skills.

Transform your business into a knowledge-driven organisation.

Trust is the core component of managing knowledge.

U

Understand the importance of managing knowledge to your business.

Unleash energy as an effective driver.

V

Values underpin your organisational culture.

Vision of your organisation should reflect the importance of managing knowledge.

W

Winning organisations are best practice organisations.

X

Xylem or supporting tissue of your organisation is constituted by knowledge.

Y

Your leadership, enthusiasm and attitude matter most in transforming your organisation.

Z

Zeal and zest of your employees should be leveraged to become knowledge-driven organisation.

Further Reading

Barker, Mike (2000) 'Knowledge management: best practice', *Personnel Today*, 29 February.

Bokin, Jim (1999) *Smart Business: How Knowledge Communities Can Revolutionize Your Company*, Free Press, New York.

Bukowitz, Wendi and Williams, Ruth L. (1999) *The Knowledge Management Fieldbook*, Pearson Education, Harlow.

Coles, Margaret (1999) 'Knowing is succeeding', *Director*, 52 (8, Mar).

Coles, Margaret (2000) 'Sharing knowledge boosts efficiency', *Sunday Times*, April 30.

Davenport, Thomas H., De Long, David W. and Beers, Michael C. (1998) 'Successful knowledge management projects', *Sloan Management Review*, 39 (2, Winter).

Dixon, Nancy M. (2000) *Common Knowledge: How Companies Thrive by Sharing What They Know*, Harvard Business School Press, Boston, MA.

Gladstone, Bryan (2000) *From Know How to Knowledge: The Essential Guide to Understanding and Implementing Knowledge Management*, Industrial Society, London.

Kermally, Sultan (1996) *Total Management Thinking*, Butterworth Heinemann, Oxford.

Kermally, Sultan (2000) *New Economy Energy: Unleashing Knowledge for Competitive Advantage*, John Wiley, Chichester.

Koulopoulos, Thomas M. and Frappaolo, Carl (1999) *Smart Things to Know About Knowledge Management*, Capstone, Oxford.

KPMG Management Consulting (1998) *The Power of Knowledge: A Business Guide to Knowledge Management*, KPMG, London.

Lucas, Erika (2000) 'Creating a give and take culture', *Professional Manager*, 9 (3, May).

Nonaka, I. and Takeuchi, H. (1995) *The Knowledge-Creating Company: How Japanese Companies Create the Dynamics of Innovation*, Oxford University Press, Oxford.

Pfeffer, Jeffrey and Sutton, Robert (1999) *The Knowing Doing Gap: How Smart Companies Turn Knowledge into Action*, Harvard Business School Press, Boston, MA.

Prigg, Mark, 'It's simple when you know how', *Sunday Times*, May 14.

Rock, Stuart (ed.) (2000) *Business Guide to Liberating Knowledge*, Caspian, London.

Skryme, David J. (1999) *Knowledge Networking: Creating the Collaborative Enterprise*, Butterworth Heinemann, Oxford.

Stewart, T. (1997) *Intellectual Capital: The New Wealth of Organizations*, Nicholas Brealey, London.

Webb, Sylvia P. (1998) *Knowledge Management Lynchpin of Change: Some Practical Guidelines*, Aslib, London.

10 Useful Web Sites

1 www.fitforthefuture.org.uk
2 www.dti.gov.uk
3 www.cabinet-office.gov.uk
4 www.ft.com
5 www.businessexcellence.co.uk
6 www.best-in-class.com
7 www.apqc.org
8 www.clicktools.com
9 www.prosci.com
10 www.brint.com

References

Barrow, Colin, Brown, Robert and Clarke, Liz (1992) *The Business Growth Handbook*, Kogan Page, London.

CBI and KPMG Consulting (2001) The Quiet Revolution, CBI/KPMG Consulting/London Business School, London, February.

Churchman, Charles West (1971) *The Design of Inquiring Systems: Basic Concepts of Systems and Organization*, Basic Books, New York.

Commission of the European Communities (1999) *The Competitiveness of European Enterprises in the Face of Globalisation: How It Can Be Encouraged*, COM(98)718Final, Brussels, 20 January.

Daft, Richard (1999) *Management*, Thomson Learning, London.

Drucker, Peter (1954) *The Practice of Management*, Harper & Row, New York.

Drucker, Peter (1985) *Innovation and Entrepreneurship*, Butterworth Heinemann, Oxford.

Furber, Rob (2000) 'Human rights', *Marketing Week*, October 26, pp. 93–4.

Hamel, Gary (n.d.) Microsoft *Digital Britain*, 3, p. 12.

Hammer, Michael and Champy, James (1993) *Reengineering the Corporation: A Manifesto for Business Revolution*, HarperBusiness, New York.

Kaplan, Robert and Norton, David (1996) *The Balanced Scorecard: Translating Strategy into Action*, Harvard Business School Press, Boston, MA.

Kermally, Sultan (1996) *Total Management Thinking*, Butterworth Heinemann, Oxford.

Nonaka, I. and Takeuchi, H. (1995) *The Knowledge-Creating Company: How Japanese Companies Create the Dynamics of Innovation*, Oxford University Press, Oxford.

Senge, Peter (1998) 'The leader's new work: building learning organisations', in Segal-Horn, Susan (ed.), *The Strategy Reader*, Blackwell, Oxford.

Witthaus, Michele (2000) 'Data overload', *Marketing Week*, 26 October.

Index